W9-BMG-299

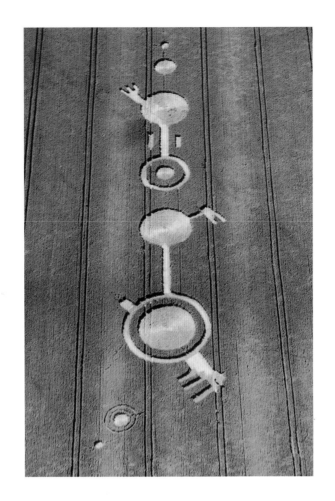

THE WORLD OF THE
UNEXPLAINED

THE WORLD OF THE
UNEXPLAINED

AN ILLUSTRATED GUIDE
TO THE PARANORMAL

Janet and Colin Bord

BLANDFORD

A BLANDFORD BOOK

First published in the UK 1998 by Blandford
A Cassell Imprint

CASSELL PLC
Wellington House, 125 Strand
London WC2R 0BB

Text © 1998 Janet & Colin Bord

The rights of Janet Bord and Colin Bord to be
identified as the authors of this work have been
asserted by them under the provisions of the UK
Copyright, Designs and Patents Act 1988.

Distributed in the United States by
Sterling Publishing Co., Inc., 387 Park Avenue
South, New York, NY 10016-8810

British Library Cataloguing-in-Publication Data
A Cataloguing-in-Publication Data entry for this
title is available from the British Library
ISBN 0-7137-2746-2

Designed by Richard Carr
Printed in the United States

CONTENTS

INTRODUCTION

THE WORLD OF the unexplained has always been with us; despite continual scientific discoveries, the human race is never going to be in the situation where there is nothing left to find out. Nevertheless we continually strive for that goal, and it is possible that this unending curiosity will eventually bring about the annihilation of the human race. Nevertheless, curiosity is a basic human reaction when faced with mystery, and it is natural to explore and try to make sense of the apparently inexplicable happenings that are continually reported.

Interest in the unknown ebbs and flows, and it may be that, as each new generation matures, a fascination with mysteries takes hold, only to decline after a year or two until the next generation rediscovers it. Sometimes the pattern is influenced by anniversaries. In 1997 it was the fiftieth anniversary of the alleged UFO crash at Roswell, New Mexico, USA, and of Kenneth Arnold's UFO sighting over Mount Rainier in Washington State, and this joint anniversary triggered a massive interest in UFOs. Now, the approach of a new millennium will inevitably produce apprehension as we move from the known and familiar into the unknown, another 1,000 years stretching away into a distant future that will remain unknowable to us.

The unpredictable future is similar to death: we all have to go there, but we are never sure what awaits us, and that naturally makes us nervous. Undaunted, we try to do the impossible: to predict the future. Some people also try, through mediums, to contact the dead, sometimes in the hope of learning what death is going to

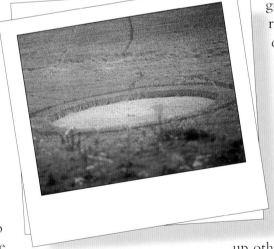

be like. There are also people who claim to have had near-death experiences, with brief glimpses of an afterlife before rushing back to the reality of the here and now.

Whenever a new mystery arises, such as the recent crop circles in the UK, the media's need for novelty and sensation result in it being widely reported, and human curiosity then takes over, especially with those people in whom a chord is struck. One problem is that few devotees of each new mystery have much knowledge of the mysteries which have been recorded earlier, and so they cannot examine the new events in the light of what has gone before. So the devotees tend to divide into two camps: those who are really seeking sensationalism and entertainment, and whose interest is easily satisfied by the media's mostly superficial treatment, and those who are prepared to delve more deeply, to read the books and articles published by earlier generations of researchers in order to place a mystery in its wider context and more fully understand what is taking place. The new generation then investigates, researches and makes new conjectures, and writes its own books, the best of which are incorporated into the existing body of knowledge. Each new wave of interest also sparks new magazines, television programmes and films, as well as books, and thus the 'unknown' thrives and gains momentum until the mass audience is sated and takes up other enthusiasms.

We have been involved with the world of mysteries for over 30 years, each of us coming into the field separately because of our interest in UFOs, which was sparked during the 1960s when UK sighting reports were at an all-time high; it was through our interest in UFOs that we met. We began to write books and collect photographs during the 1970s. The Fortean Picture Library was born in 1978, when Bob Rickard, editor of the successful magazine *Fortean Times*, handed us Doc Shiels' famous photograph of the Loch Ness Monster and suggested we look after it. Since then we have collected many thousands of photographs and the more we collect, the more intriguing the whole field becomes.

We are very aware that a proportion of our photographs that claim to depict mysteries are probably fakes; indeed, that first photograph of 'Nessie' is itself questioned. It is easy enough for someone to suggest that a photograph is a hoax, but usually impossible to prove it; hoaxers are notoriously slow to come forward and admit what they have done. Hoaxing is rarely done for financial gain. Sometimes it is done to show how gullible people are, but often it is done simply for the thrill of doing it and successfully fooling people. The hoaxer possesses a piece of knowledge that is held by no one else. Others may have their suspicions, but the hoaxer is the only one who really knows. Of course, there are also photographs that appear to show mysterious events which are a hoax by the person or people involved rather than by the photographer. Again the hoaxer is the only one who can be sure what is happening, although others might have their suspicions. The art of metal-bending is an example of this. Is it done by the power of psychokinesis (PK, or mind over matter) or by sleight of hand? Ghosts too can be faked, and we have even produced our own ghostly

photographs (although of course we have never tried to pass them off as genuine images of something inexplicable; they are a demonstration of what *can* be done rather than real hoaxes).

In fact, it is true to say that every mystery can be explained away as a hoax or a misidentification, and there are sceptics who do this continually. However, such people are at the opposite extreme to the 'true believers' and could be called 'true unbelievers': they are determined to find prosaic explanations for every mystery that arises, almost as if they are afraid to accept that we are not in control of every aspect of our world. The true sceptic retains an open mind, intrigued by the facts as they appear to be, yet aware that often things are not what they seem. The true sceptic is neither a believer nor a disbeliever, but seeks explanations for apparent mysteries. Yet he/she is also willing to acknowledge the genuinely inexplicable when, as occasionally does happen, such a thing presents itself.

There are probably very few genuinely mysterious photographs. That is the conclusion we have reached after more than 20 years of collecting them. However we cannot be 100 per cent sure which ones are genuine. We are, of course, intrigued by the origins of our photographs, but it is not our role to investigate them or to pronounce on their reliability (although we have our suspicions as to some of the hoaxes). As collectors of mysterious pictures, we see our role as simply to present them, with such facts as are known to us. The rest is up to you.

Janet & Colin Bord
North Wales, January 1998

MYSTERY
ANIMALS

INTRODUCTION

EVEN THOUGH THERE seems to be no part of planet Earth where humans have not set foot, and the truly wild areas are diminishing at an alarming rate, it remains a fact that we do not have a complete record of all the animals that share the planet with us. While this seems feasible in regard to small creatures, it might seem unlikely that anything larger than, say, a fox would remain undetected until the end of the twentieth century. Nevertheless this is the case. The major discovery of this century has been the okapi (a short-necked giraffe living in the Congo forest), which was found almost 100 years ago. More recently, in 1992, the first traces of the Vu Quang ox were found in a nature reserve on the Vietnam–Laos border. There have been many more finds of totally new, though smaller, creatures and also plenty of rediscoveries of ones thought to be extinct. Other 'extinct' animals are also likely to re-emerge before too long, the thylacine of Tasmania being especially hotly tipped to make a comeback, judging by all the sighting reports.

Exciting as all these discoveries may be, the major prey of cryptozoologists (people who study mystery animals) is rather more elusive. It comprises the 'monsters' of the animal kingdom which are rumoured to exist but for which little, if any, hard evidence has yet been found. Into this category come creatures such as the Loch Ness Monster, the Yeti, and the Bigfoot or Sasquatch. Many sightings have been reported, but no corpses have been obtained and the few photographs that have been taken are inconclusive and usually controversial.

If any of these giant creatures do exist, they are likely to be prehistoric survivals. It is not impossible that some animals from the age of dinosaurs may have survived. One such, which has definitely been identified, is the coelacanth, a 5ft (1.5m) long, deepwater fish discovered in the sea off South Africa in 1938. However, there is a considerable difference between a 5ft (1.5m) long fish from an inaccessible habitat and a 7ft (2.1m) tall man-beast living in the North American forests! The Bigfoot allegedly has cousins in other parts of the world – the Yeti in the Himalayas, the Almas in the Caucasus Mountains (former USSR), the Yowie in Australia; man-beasts have reportedly been seen in many remote corners of the world. If they do genuinely exist, they may be the survivors of early ape-men such as *Gigantopithecus*.

Hominids are not the only giants to have been reported, however. The existence of water-dwelling dinosaurs such as the plesiosaur might account for sightings of the Loch Ness Monster and other lake monsters around the world, while the ocean could be home to formidable giants such as pliosaurs, mosasaurs and thalattosuchians. Water monsters are often reported but the sightings are usually fleeting and reliable photographic evidence is virtually non-existent. Until carcases in good condition are obtained, the existence of prehistoric giants remains pure speculation. In fact some carcases have been found: they are washed up on remote beaches from time to time and, although none of them has yet proved to be from one of the prehistoric giants, they have at least shown that creatures such as giant squids do exist.

Unlikely as it may seem, there are also persistent reports of giant birds, including some that may be prehistoric survivors. Sightings of pterosaurs (flying reptiles) in Texas, USA, may sound like the stuff of horror fiction, yet there have been several such reports in recent years, like that made by a man, driving an ambulance in September 1983, who saw a creature with a 5–6ft (1.5–1.8m) wingspan whose thin body was clad in a rough-textured hide rather than feathers and which had a tail like a fin. He stopped and watched as it skimmed the grass and flew away. Amerindian mythology tells of the Thunderbird – a giant bird of prey – and there have also been reports of giant birds picking up children, as happened in 1977, in Illinois, USA, to ten-year-old Marlon Lowe. The creature carried his 65lb (29.5kg) weight for 30–40ft (9–12m) before dropping him again. The black, vulture-like bird, which had an 8–10ft (2.4–3m) wingspan, was never identified.

Other monster survivors rumoured to have been seen in recent times include the woolly mammoth, the diprotodon (a possible identification for the Australian bunyip, a mysterious aquatic mammal), the moa (a giant New Zealand bird) and the mokele-mbembe (a water monster hiding in the Congo jungles). The list could continue indefinitely for there is no shortage of people coming forward to report sightings of weird and wonderful things. The problem, as stated earlier, is that there is little real evidence: no carcases, no clear photographs. How much reliance can be placed on eyewitness testimony? It is probable that witnesses are usually honest and genuinely believe that they have seen something strange but, in the heat of the moment, people can

be mistaken about what they see, and objects can seem to be larger than they really are if the witness is startled or frightened. The difficulty is distinguishing between those reports that are really misidentifications of some known creature and those which are truly mysterious.

As if this were not complicated enough, there is another dimension to consider: the possibility that some of the monsters people claim to have seen may be non-physical in nature. If the weirder Bigfoot-sighting reports are to be believed, this is a monster with the ability to disappear into thin air! There have also been suggestions that other monsters, such as Nessie and the airborne giants, may also be ghosts rather than living creatures. As with all non-physical beings, because there is no testable evidence these concepts remain interesting but unproven.

Monsters and mystery animals have always been with us. Mythology contains some very weird ones, such as the chimera (a lion in front, a dragon behind and a she-goat in the middle), the manticora (like a lion with a man's head), the centaur (part horse and part man) and Pegasus, the winged horse, as well as the more familiar dragons and unicorns. Some of these were based on real creatures, but some were imaginary, and the same still holds true today. If only we could determine for certain which of our twentieth-century monsters are real and which imaginary. On the other hand, perhaps not – our world would be the poorer if we could no longer believe in (and be in awe of) the Loch Ness Monster and Bigfoot.

LOCH NESS MONSTER

Each year there are several sightings of something strange in Loch Ness in Scotland, and many people believe that it could be a prehistoric monster, such as a plesiosaur. From time to time someone manages to take a photograph that shows something unusual — a disturbance in the water, or what appears to be a head and neck sticking out — but however exciting these photographs may be, they are no use as evidence. What is needed is a live monster, or at least a body, and no body or even part of one has ever been found. This is not surprising because the lake is about 25 miles (40km) long, 1 mile (1.6km) wide, and up to 900ft (274m) deep in places.

R.K.Wilson's famous photograph of the Loch Ness Monster, taken in 1934.

THE MOST FAMOUS of all the Loch Ness Monster photographs (shown opposite) is the one taken in April 1934 by R. K. Wilson, a London surgeon. He was on holiday at the loch and had with him a camera that used glass plates, with a telephoto lens for game-bird photography. After an all-night drive, he stopped beside the loch near Invermoriston and walked down to the water. Seeing a disturbance 200–300yd (180–275m) out, and an animal's head appearing, he went to fetch his camera and took four photographs. He had the plates developed in nearby Inverness; two were found to be blank but the other two bore distinct images of what appeared to be the head and neck of an unknown creature.

In the 60 years since the photographs were taken, some people have accepted them as evidence for the existence of the monster while others have interpreted them as something else: the tail of a diving otter, or a bird, for example. Other people believe that Wilson was involved in a clever hoax. Until his death in 1969 Wilson refused to discuss the photographs with the press, stating only that he had photographed an object moving in Loch Ness. In August 1992, 86-year-old Lambert Wilson (no relation to the photographer) claimed that he was the 'monster' in the famous photograph. He said he had bought a sea-snake head from a joke-shop and turned it into a realistic monster head, then swam underwater carrying the head above him, watching the reaction of people on the shore through peepholes he had cut in the neck. He believed this was the 'monster' which R. K. Wilson had photographed.

However, a new claim was publicized early in 1994 – that the monster in Wilson's photograph was a model made from plastic wood and attached to a clockwork toy submarine. Christian Spurling claimed to be the model-maker as he lay on his deathbed late in 1993. He also said that Wilson had helped him with the joke. This was because Spurling's stepfather had been humiliated when he had identified some large footprints on the loch shore as being those of the monster; in fact, they were a hoax and had been made with a hippopotamus's foot. (The hippo was dead, of course! Its foot had been made into an ashtray.)

Some people accepted without question that Spurling's claim was true, but others are not so sure, including cryptozoologist Dr Karl Shuker, who has found numerous problems with the details of the claim. Firstly, it seems that plastic wood had not been invented in 1934. Secondly, it is unlikely that a toy submarine could have supported a model head and neck without overbalancing and, if the submarine had been weighted to make it more stable, it would have sunk to the bottom of the lake. Thirdly, detailed calculations using weather information suggest that the neck was about 4ft (1.2m) tall, not 1ft (30cm) as claimed by the hoaxer. Fourthly, the second photograph taken by Wilson looks very different from the one usually seen, which is impossible if the same model was photographed both times. There are also other problems with the hoax claim, so much so that it becomes less likely the more it is studied in detail. So perhaps Wilson's photographs are genuine after all!

THE ONLY OTHER clear photograph of a neck and head was obtained in 1977 by Anthony Shiels, who was at the time watching for the monster from the ruined walls of Urquhart Castle. 'Doc' Shiels (as he is more usually known) is an artist, although he also has many other talents, including those of magician and Punch and Judy man. Wizard and psychic entertainer are two more facets of his personality, and he was actually at Loch Ness as part of an attempt to conjure up water monsters. His successful sighting on 21 May was unfortunately not witnessed by anyone else. According to his own description of what happened, a sleek head broke the surface of the loch . . .

> . . . rather less than a hundred yards away . . . the part of the neck showing above the water-line must have been around 4 or 5ft long . . .

The colour of the animal was greenish brown, with a paler underside. Skin texture, smooth and glossy. The animal was visible for no more than 4 or 5 seconds. It held itself very upright, very still, except for a turning of the head and a straightening of the neck before it sank very smoothly, below the surface. It had powerful neck muscles.

Doc managed to fire off two frames during those few seconds, one of which was unfortunately lost. The other is shown above. Doc was also closely involved with the photographs of Morgawr (see p.29) and, indeed, he has been accused of hoaxing them, an accusation which has been extended to include his photographs of Nessie. However, he maintains that the events took place as he described them.

INEVITABLY, EVERY PHOTOGRAPH purporting to show the Loch Ness Monster is subjected to very close scrutiny and an alternative explanation is usually forthcoming. The latest in a series of intriguing but inconclusive photographs were taken on Sunday 11 August 1996 by Austin Hepburn, who teaches art at a school in Inverness not far from the loch. He had gone to the loch in order to try out his new camera and, while he was driving up a road that overlooks the loch, decided to stop and take some pictures. It was then that he noticed something moving through the water. It was not a boat; indeed there was no movement from boats or anything else on that hot summer's day. All that was moving was the 'something' in the water. Hepburn took six photographs altogether, including the one shown above. They show that the object was moving across the water, but he couldn't get any closer to it because there was a field between him and the lake. Hepburn is an experienced fisherman and he could

tell that the moving object was something he did not recognize. Eventually it went under water and the lake was still again. Austin discovered that it had also been seen by other people, and some Canadian tourists had videoed something about ¼ mile (0.4km) along the loch earlier in the afternoon.

Inevitably, the disturbance on the water has been described as nothing more than a boat wake, even though Hepburn claims that no boats were moving. The most common explanations for sightings of the 'monster' are boats and boat wakes, rotting vegetation and dead wood floating in the water, swimming deer, otters, water birds – and, of course, hoaxes. Nevertheless there are many people who cannot agree that these are the only explanations and, despite the failure to find conclusive proof of a monster after 40 years of research at Loch Ness, we still cannot deny the possibility that the Loch Ness Monster may be alive and well, and living (usually) deep under the water.

LAKE MONSTERS WORLD-WIDE

Although the Loch Ness Monster is the most famous lake monster, there are many more in all continents, if the sighting reports are to be believed.

Canada has many monster-haunted lakes, Okanagan Lake (below) in British Columbia being perhaps the one from which most reports come. There were tales of monsters

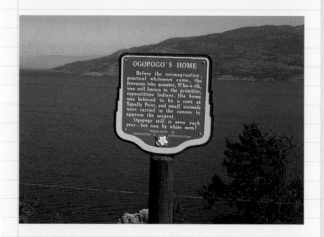

in Indian lore when the first white settlers arrived in 1860, and the monster (nicknamed 'Ogopogo') has been regularly reported since then. One report described it as being 30-70ft (9-21m) long, with a dark, sleek body, 1-2ft (30-60cm) thick, and a horse-like head. Unfortunately there are no good photographs of Ogopogo - so far as we are aware - and the same applies to most lake monsters. Whether this is simply because the creatures rarely show themselves above water, so that photographs purporting to be of lake monsters show only disturbances on the water, or whether it is because the creatures simply don't exist and the disturbances people see are attributable to something else, cannot easily be decided. What is clear is that sighting reports persist.

IN THE NORTHERN hemisphere – along with Canada and the USA, Scotland and Ireland – Scandinavia, with its many lakes, also has its fair share of lake monsters. Further east, there are occasional reports from Siberian lakes; if the area was more densely populated, there would doubtless be more. The drawing below shows a monster seen in Lake Khaiyr by a biologist, N. F. Gladkikh, in 1964. Early one morning, he saw the creature on the lake shore, eating grass. It had a small head, a long, gleaming neck, and a huge, bluish-black body with a fin along its spine. Although he was a biologist, Gladkikh did not recognize the animal and rushed off to fetch his colleagues, members of a scientific expedition. They quickly grabbed guns and cameras, but the monster had gone, leaving only trampled grass behind. Later, three other members of the team saw a head appear in the middle of the lake with the dorsal fin also showing. The monster was lashing the water with its long tail and sending waves across the

lake. Reports of monsters in northern lakes are often explained as being sightings of large fish, such as sturgeon, but we have never before heard of a fish that climbs out of its habitat to feed on grass! Two pilots who saw creatures in the lake in 1942 described them as giant newts.

LAKE MONSTERS HAVE also been reported from further east, for example in Lake Ikeda, in Japan. Witnesses there describe a fast-moving creature with at least two black humps; seen by 20 people in September 1978, it was said to be 60–90ft (18–27m) long. Disturbances in the lake have also been captured on video – but sceptics believe that the sightings may be caused by unusual wave formations being bounced off the shore. The representation of 'Issie', as the creature has become known, that has been erected on the shore of Lake Ikeda (see the photograph below) displays rather more of her than has so far been observed 'in the flesh', and therefore is somewhat fanciful to say the least.

ALTHOUGH FEWER REPORTS come from lakes in the African and South American continents, this may be because these areas are often remote and lacking easy contact with the outside world. However, there are enough reports to show that monsters also inhabit southern hemisphere lakes. Many reports could be attributable to known creatures seen under unusual circumstances, but sometimes the reports are definitely of something strange. The best example must be the creature known as mokele-mbembe, which is said to live in the lakes and rivers of the Likouala swamps that cover about 55,000 square miles (143,000km²) of the African Congo. Numerous expeditions in search of the monster have been made to the area in recent years, but no conclusive proof of its existence has yet been obtained. Native eyewitnesses have described their encounters with the monster, which has a long neck and was seen to make footprints the size of a dinner-plate when it came out of the water and onto a sandbar. Its long tail dragged behind and made a trench in the sand. It has four legs and one witness estimated the creature to be about 30ft (9m) long from head to tip of tail and up to 6ft (1.8m) tall. Although it appears to be a herbivore, the monster can be dangerous, coming to the surface under dugout canoes and overturning them before killing the occupants by biting them and hitting them with its tail, although it does not eat them.

The painting shown here is based on the eyewitness descriptions, and the details given by witnesses have led some researchers to believe that mokele-mbembe might be a small sauropod dinosaur or a giant, long-necked monitor lizard. It has also been more cautiously identified as an elephant with raised trunk crossing the rivers, or a giant turtle. Even if mokele-mbembe were to be identified, there still remains another mystery animal in the same area: the emela-ntouka ('killer of elephants'), which is another herbivorous water monster, this time with a sharp horn on its snout which it uses to attack elephants and buffaloes. One possible identification is a ceratopsian dinosaur but, as with mokele-mbembe, substantial hard evidence, preferably in the form of a carcase, is needed before this mystery can be solved.

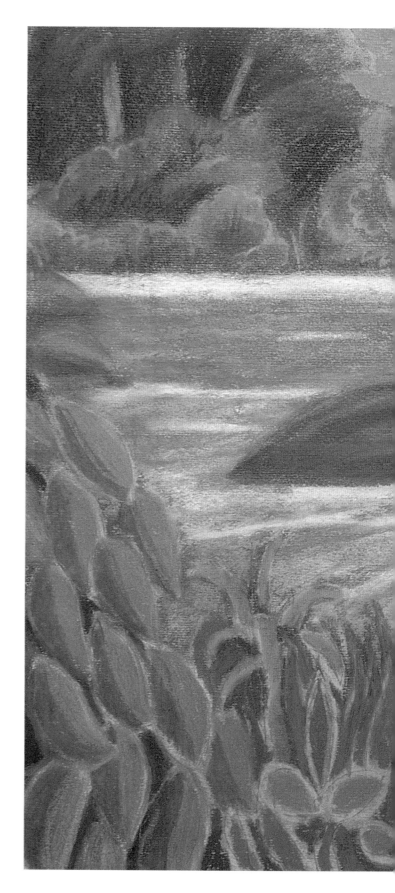

MYTHICAL MONSTERS

Many weird and wonderful creatures have emerged from ancient mythological texts, some of which have already been mentioned (see p.13), but probably the best known are dragons and unicorns. Dragons were known worldwide, appearing in many different forms and living in the sea as well as on land. They were often serpentine, sometimes with legs, sometimes winged, sometimes breathing fire, and were often depicted being slain by St George or some other brave knight.

THE WANTLEY DRAGON (see the picture below) was killed near Sheffield, UK, by the knight More of More Hall. The story is a familiar one in British folklore. The dragon lived in

a den and came out from time to time to devastate the countryside and kill people and livestock. Those who survived its depredations sought the help of the local knight, who agreed to take on the challenge. He obtained a spiked suit of armour and, after a few pots of ale to give him courage, he hid in the well where the dragon went to drink. As it approached, he jumped out and bashed it on the nose. This annoyed the dragon, and a fearsome battle resulted which lasted two days and a night. Unable to kill the dragon in fair combat, More finally finished it off by kicking it up the backside with his spiked boot. The death is graphically described in the last verse of a seventeenth-century broadside ballad:

> Murder! murder! the Dragon cryed,
> Alack! alack! for grief;
> Had you but miss't that place you would
> Have done me no mischief.
> Then his head he shak't,
> Trembled and quaik't,
> And down he layed, and cried;
> First on one knee,
> Then on back tumbled he,
> So groaned, kick't, burst, and dyed.

RAGONS MAY HAVE had their origins in prehistoric monsters and an image linking these two concepts is the dragon, or sirrush (see the photograph on the right) on the Ishtar Gate at Babylon, which dates from the reign of King Nebuchadnezzar II in the sixth century BC. After the fall of Babylon c.39 BC, the gate was buried in the sands of Mesopotamia until it was rediscovered at the beginning of this century. The three animals portrayed on the gate were a bull, a lion and the dragon. The first two are real animals, so why not the third? Yet it resembles no known living animal. However, it does have features that remind zoologists of the sauropod dinosaurs – the same species that has been put forward as a possible contender to explain the mokele-mbembe of the African Congo. Is it too far-fetched to suggest that a living dinosaur was captured in the Congo and taken back to Babylon, where it became immortalized on the magnificent Ishtar Gate?

OULD THE FABULOUS unicorn, with its long, thin, upward-pointing horn, also have been a real animal? Seventeenth-century explorers reported seeing them in places such as Abyssinia and Tibet, but all the so-called 'unicorn' horns which were brought home in reality came from the narwhal, a species of whale with one long tusk. However, there once lived in Europe a strange antelope with two upward-pointing horns which were very close together and which probably, from a distance, looked like one horn. It is known as *Procamptoceras brivatense* and it became extinct before humans moved into Europe – or so it is believed. If this creature did survive for longer, and was occasionally seen, it is not impossible that descriptions of it were passed down through the generations. Sadly, the unicorn shown here is only a model, prepared for an exhibition of legendary animals at the Zoological Museum in Copenhagen, Denmark.

WEREWOLVES

People in the past, and even today, have claimed to be able to change into animal form, and the werewolf is the best-known man-into-animal transformation.

A FAMOUS HISTORICAL example of a supposed werewolf was the Beast of the Gevaudan, which terrorized the area of Clermont-Ferrand in France in the eighteenth century. Looking like a large wolf with reddish hair, it attacked and killed people. Soldiers killed over 100 wolves in a month, but the attacks continued and people began to believe it must be a werewolf. One day a large beast with reddish hair was shot and killed, and a girl's shoulder-bone was found in its stomach, but the carcase rotted before a proper examination could be made. Recently, however, it has been suggested that the creature was in fact a striped hyena and not a werewolf at all.

Jean Grenier was a teenage boy in eighteenth-century France who claimed to be a werewolf. When wolf attacks were reported in his home area, he claimed responsibility and, when he was arrested, he told the court that: 'When I was ten or eleven years old, my neighbour, Duthillaire, introduced me, in the depths of the forest, to a M. de la Forest,

The werewolf of Eschenbach, 1685.

a black man who signed me with his skin. From that time I have run about the country as a wolf.' Because he knew details of the murders which no one else but the murderer could know, he was found guilty and imprisoned for life but, being obviously mentally ill, he was held in a monastery, where he died aged 20 years.

Modern examples of people who have not only believed themselves to be werewolves but have, in that guise, attacked and killed humans are rare. However, there are on record a number of cases of recent sightings of fearsome beings, apparently half human and half wolf, which may perhaps be classified as werewolves. One such dated from 1888, and the events took place in Merionethshire in North Wales. A professor on holiday in the area found a huge, dog-like skull in a lake while fishing, and took it back to the cottage where he, his wife and friend were staying. That evening, while only the woman was in the cottage, she heard scratching noises at the kitchen door and saw a horrible face at the window. It had paws like hands, red eyes, and a face that seemed to be part wolf and part man. It prowled

The Gevaudan Beast with its paw on a dead man.

around the cottage trying to get in but, by the time the men returned, it had gone. Later that night it returned and when the men, armed with a gun, opened the door to confront it, it ran off and they saw it disappear into the lake. Next day the professor threw the skull into the lake and the werewolf was never seen again.

An equally dramatic sequence of events was reported in the 1970s. It began with the unearthing of two strange stone heads, smaller than tennis balls, in a garden at Hexham, Northumberland, UK. Their presence in the house was followed by poltergeist-like activity and a creature 'half man, half beast' was seen padding down the stairs in a neighbouring house. Celtic expert Dr Anne Ross took the heads to her home in southern England, where she too experienced an unwelcome visitor, which was seen both by herself and other members of the family. It was 6ft (1.8m) tall, with black fur; the upper part seemed like a wolf, while the lower part looked human. It was usually seen on the stairs where, halfway down, it would vault over the banister and thud softly onto the floor. The evil presence in the house seemed to have spread from the Hexham heads to all the Celtic stone heads in Dr Ross's collection, and it only departed when all the heads were removed from the house.

There are people around today who believe that humans can appear as animals. In 1977 an American psychiatry journal described a 49-year-old woman who had delusions of changing into a wolf. She would fall into a trance and say:

> I am a wolf of the night, I am a wolf-woman of the day . . . I have claws, teeth, fangs, hair, and anguish is my prey at night. I am what I am, and will always roam the earth long after death.

The woman was given treatment, which lessened her attacks. Psychiatrists believe there are various causes for this illness, including schizophrenia, hysteria and brain disease.

A nineteenth-century engraving depicting a werewolf being chased by a crowd, headed by a monk with a crucifix.

A psychiatric explanation would hardly account, however, for the following case reported in the Malaysian Press in 1979. According to this report a thief who was trying to enter a house in the Jasin Pantai District of Kampung Serkam Timor had suddenly turned into a dog. The animal was captured and imprisoned at the Air Keroh Veterinary Office but, before tests could be carried out to determine whether or not it was a real dog, it mysteriously disappeared from the cell where it was being held.

Its absence was discovered when a worker went in to feed the dog. He reported that the rope which had been tied around its neck had not been undone, nor had the door and the lock been tampered with. It was not known how the dog had escaped and the suggestion was that, being a supernatural creature, it had simply dematerialized.

A werewolf kidnaps a woman.

SEA MONSTERS

Reports of sea monsters go back into antiquity and it is hardly surprising that people should always have believed the vast oceans to be a home for unimaginable monsters.

IN THE EARLY days, sea monsters were depicted as being gigantic and extremely dangerous to sailors, as shown in the drawing below, which comes from a map of the northern lands, published in 1539 by Olaus Magnus. Magnus was a Swedish archbishop who, a few years later, wrote a book quoting the stories he had heard.

MORE RECENTLY, THE depictions of sea monsters, like that of the giant squid opposite, have become more realistic. This giant squid was seen off Tenerife on 30 November 1861. The commander of the French gunboat *Alecton* was curious about a large, floating mass and, when he realized it was a giant 'octopus' (there was confusion at that time between squids and octopuses), he tried to capture it as it swam away. Bullets seemed not to affect it and so the crew managed to get a harpoon into it. A noose was put around the body, but it slipped and the body broke away from the tail, so all they saved was the tip of the tail. Nevertheless, they were able to estimate that the squid was 15–18ft (4.5–5.5m) long from tail to beak, not counting its arms, which were 5–6ft (1.5–1.8m) long. Its staring eyes were said to be like plates and its mouth was 18in (45cm) across.

DESPITE MANY REPORTED sightings all around the world, the only pictures of sea monsters are graphic drawings like the examples shown on the previous two pages. There are no photographs in existence which are 100 per cent reliable, so far as we are aware, and the two printed here both have question-marks hanging over them. The photograph on this page was taken on 12 December 1964 in Stonehaven Bay off Hook Island, Australia, by Robert Le Serrec, a French photographer who had sailed to Australia with his wife and family and then been shipwrecked on the Great Barrier Reef. He was spending a few months on Hook Island and, according to his story, he and his wife were crossing Stonehaven Bay in a motor boat to fetch fresh water when they saw something lying on the bottom of the sea. It was like a giant tadpole: a huge head and a thin body about 30ft (9m) long. They circled it for half an hour, filming it with a ciné camera, before going underwater to get some closer shots. They went within 20ft (6m) of the monster and were later able to describe it in detail. When it opened its mouth and turned towards them, they fled. By the time they reached the safety of their boat, it had gone.

Cryptozoologist Bernard Heuvelmans discussed this sighting at length in his important book *In the Wake of the Sea-Serpents*, and was sceptical about its truthfulness, because Le Serrec had described the creature's eyes as pointing upwards, which

Heuvelmans felt was unlikely. Could the men have actually seen something like a deflated weather balloon, or similar large piece of fabric? Or might they even have concocted a hoax? There were various details emerging about Le Serrec which did not inspire confidence – and the underwater shots, which might have been expected to provide closer detail, and therefore confirmation of the animal's reality, turned out to be fuzzy.

THE TRUTH ABOUT two photographs of an English sea monster has turned out to be equally hard to obtain. 1975–76 was a busy time down in Cornwall, UK, where numerous people reported sightings of a sea monster off Falmouth. Early in 1976 an anonymous photographer, who gave the name 'Mary F.', claimed to have obtained two photographs (one of which is shown above) of the creature, which was by now known as 'Morgawr', meaning 'sea giant' in the ancient Cornish language. In her letter to the local newspaper, 'Mary F.' said that the monster was only visible for a few seconds, but she estimated that the body was 15–18ft (4.5–5.5m) long.

It looked like an elephant waving its trunk, but the trunk was a long neck with a small head on the end, like a snake's head. It had humps on the back which moved in a funny way. The colour was black or very dark brown, and the skin seemed to be like a sealion's . . . the animal frightened me. I would not like to see it any closer. I do not like the way it moved when swimming.

Doc Shiels, who in 1977 was to photograph the Loch Ness Monster (see p.16), was living in Falmouth at the time when Morgawr was making her presence felt and claimed two sightings himself. On the second occasion he was with David Clarke, a magazine editor who was photographing Doc for a feature article. As they walked by the estuary, they both saw 'a small dark head poking out of the water' and, as it moved closer, they saw that 'the greenish black head was supported on a long arched neck, more slender than that of a seal'. The head was ugly, like a big snail's head with little stalks or horns, and Doc estimated that the animal was no more than 15ft (4.5m) long. David Clarke hurriedly fitted a telephoto lens to his camera and could see the magnified image of the creature as he fired off several frames. Sadly, however, he later discovered that his camera had not been winding on the film correctly, and so the pictures were double exposures. Despite the creature's frequent appearances, both during 1976 and in later years, no fully reliable photographs of Morgawr were obtained and her identity remains a mystery.

GLOBSTERS

It was Ivan T. Sanderson, the pioneering cryptozoologist (1911–73), who thought of the name 'globster' for lumps of rotting flesh found cast up on beaches around the world. Often unidentifiable, these are sometimes thought to be the remains of unknown monsters of the sea.

OF THE MANY globsters found over the years on the beaches of the world, one of the most famous was the lump of flesh, weighing around 5 tonnes, which was discovered on the beach at Anastasia Island, Florida, USA, on 30 November 1896. It measured 23ft (7m) long by 18ft (5.5m) across by 4ft (1.2m) high, and was a silvery pinkish white in colour. The remains of arms up to 32ft (9.7m) long were also seen and it was concluded that the carcase (see the photograph below) was a giant octopus measuring 200ft (60m) across the extended tentacles. All the on-site work was undertaken by Dr DeWitt Webb (pictured below), who put forward the giant octopus identification, but the scientists whom he tried to involve in his work refused to accept that the remains were anything extraordinary and for 60 years they were forgotten. However, analyses conducted since 1957 by octopus experts have confirmed that the animal was indeed a giant octopus of a kind never before seen.

A MORE RECENT carcase (see the photograph below) at first fooled people into thinking that a plesiosaur had been retrieved. The body, about 33ft (10m) long, was pulled out of the water east of Christchurch, New Zealand, on 25 April 1977, in the nets of the Japanese fishing vessel *Zuiyo Maru*. It smelled so bad that, as soon as photographs and measurements had been taken, and a few fibres saved, the rotting carcase was thrown back into the sea. The photographs were suggestive of several creatures: a sea-lion, a whale, a turtle and, the most exciting possibility of all, a plesiosaur. Eventually the saved fibres were analysed by a Tokyo University biochemist who found that they contained a type of protein found only in sharks. Although in this instance the carcase had proved to be of a known creature, it is not impossible that new species will continue to be discovered in the oceans. In fact, in 1976, a new shark was found off Hawaii. It became known as the 'megamouth shark', because of its large, wide mouth, and in following years more were found off California, Western Australia and Japan. So we should not give up hope: that elusive plesiosaur might still be found.

A lot of publicity attended the discovery of a carcase on a Tasmanian beach in August 1960. Was it merely a lump of blubber from a dead whale as some thought, or, as Jack Boote, one of the men who discovered it, said: 'They had to say it was nothing new to cover up the fact they hadn't done anything about it before ... They were too late and too slow. By the time they got there, the thing had decomposed. The thing I saw was not a whale or any part of a whale.'

Laboratory analyses were also contradictory. Zoologist Bruce Mollinson, who saw the carcase and took flesh samples, said that: 'It wasn't a whale, seal, sea elephant or squid.' He thought it was an unknown animal, possibly some sort of ray that lived in deep under-sea caverns off Tasmania. As cryptozoologist J. Richard Greenwell commented in connection with similar mystery remains: 'descriptions - and photos - are similar in all cases. All the carcases were described as tough and hard to cut, usually odourless, and very "stringy", which is often called "hairy". And curiously, all seem to be more or less unidentifiable by experts.'

DISCOVERIES AND REDISCOVERIES

Although man believes himself to be master of the Earth, the truth is that there are still vast areas of largely unexplored territory, all of them home to creatures of all sizes, some of which may never have been scientifically recorded. Also lurking there may be creatures which are known to have existed but are now believed to be extinct.

OCCASIONAL SIGHTING REPORTS keep alive the hope of rediscovery of some important animals, such as the thylacine, or Tasmanian wolf (*Thylacinus cynocephalus*). The thylacine is a marsupial – like the kangaroo – and carries its young in a pouch. It also resembles a wolf with black or chocolate-brown stripes across its back and it is from these markings that its other (confusing) name of 'Tasmanian tiger' is derived. Thousands of years ago, thylacines were widespread throughout New Guinea and Australia, but more recent records have limited its range to Tasmania. However, there have also been reported sightings in mainland Australia in recent years, which makes another unsolved mystery. In Tasmania the thylacine came to be regarded as a pest because of its reputation (perhaps ill-founded) for killing sheep, and so it was hunted into extinction in the 1930s. Thereafter, people began to search for it and, although no live or dead specimens have yet been found, there are many reported sightings, and considerable optimism that it does indeed live secretly in the Tasmanian forests. The photograph shows a captive thylacine earlier this century.

AT THE OTHER end of the spectrum are reports of monsters that defy identification and are never captured or photographed. The most recent example of this is the Chupacabras (Spanish for 'goat-sucker'), which was first reported on the island of Puerto Rico, in the Caribbean, in March 1995. People in the mountains claimed that an unseen animal was killing small farm animals, draining their blood through one small wound. Later, people described seeing a creature like a kangaroo with fangs and bulging red eyes. The painting here of the Chupacabras is based on eyewitness accounts. The search for the monster continued into 1996, although reports lessened during very cold weather, as if it had gone into hibernation. In March 1996 a farmer found 30 cocks and hens dead, and they bore puncture marks which reawakened fears that the Chupacabras was back. A boy saw a 4ft (1.2m) creature walking upright, and described its red eyes, large fangs, pointed ears, claw-like hands and dark grey body. Strange killings continued to be reported, and the panic also spread overseas to the Spanish-speaking parts of Florida and Texas, USA, probably because of media coverage. It is possible that, once the panic took hold, everyone whose livestock was killed attributed the deaths to the mysterious Chupacabras. It is also possible, of course, that some of the deaths *were* caused by a mystery predator – but so far it has not been caught, killed or even photographed.

OUT-OF-PLACE ANIMALS

Around the world, people have reported seeing animals which should not logically be there: kangaroos in Illinois and Wisconsin, pterodactyls in Texas, big cats in Australia . . . and bears, crocodiles, boars, wallabies and big cats in the UK. Wallabies are known to be living wild in colonies in various parts of the UK and there are probably big cats too. All are likely to be either escapees from private animal collections or animals that have been turned loose by their owners – a grossly irresponsible act, which is both stressful for the animal and dangerous for the public.

BLACK DOGS

IT IS POSSIBLE that some large animals seen roaming the countryside are ghostly rather than physical, especially those that are large, black and dog-like, often with glowing red eyes. Phantom black dogs crop up regularly in British folklore (and elsewhere in the world), but they are not merely legendary, for people are still seeing them today. Sometimes the black dog is a friendly animal, appearing from nowhere to escort a woman travelling alone along a dark country road. The dog seems to be a normal dog – until she puts out her hand to pat it and feels nothing at all! There have been reports of such guardians protecting women from lurking vagabonds who have also seen the phantom animals and thought them real, and have therefore kept their distance and allowed the women safe passage.

Yet sometimes the animals appear to be omens of death and so are not at all welcome to the people who unexpectedly see them.

An area of England which is particularly rich in black-dog lore is East Anglia, where the creature is known as 'Black Shuck'. His presence was believed to foretell death, or at the very least an ominous event. This was especially the case on Sunday 4 August 1577, when a black dog was seen in two churches in the area. On the morning of that day, a terrible storm arose. A black dog suddenly appeared

Title page from 'A Straunge Wunder in Bongay', the pamphlet that described the black dog seen in Bungay, Suffolk, in 1577.

in Bungay church and passed through the congregation, leaving two dead and another injured after they were touched by it. These events were described in a pamphlet published at the time.

In nearby Blythburgh church, three people died and more were injured after a black dog appeared there. He is said to have left burnt claw-marks on the church door, which can still be seen today (see the photograph opposite).

In more recent times, tales of evil black dogs have again come from the same area. In 1895, two men driving a cart along a lane at Rockland, in Norfolk, UK, suddenly encountered a huge dog. The driver kept going in spite of his companion's warning but, as the cart touched the dog, the air became alive with flames and a terrible stench, and the driver lay dead. In the same area a countryman who met Black Shuck and told him to clear off was thrown over a hedge.

Despite these frightening accounts, it would seem that phantom black dogs are more often helpful than dangerous. For example, in Lincolnshire, UK, in the 1930s, a schoolmistress who often cycled at night along a lonely lane would be accompanied by a very large dog trotting along the grass verge. She liked to know he was there. Earlier this century, and again in Lincolnshire, a woman walked to a farm one evening to visit a sick friend and was accompanied part of the way by a large, black, shaggy dog with a long tail. When she returned later in the evening, nervous at having to walk home alone, the dog rejoined her at the spot where he had left her earlier, and walked along with her until they reached the hole in the hedge where he had first appeared. She felt that he was there to protect her.

No one knows what black dogs really are, how they appear, or where they come from. Suggestions have included manifestations of the Devil, or the ghosts of dead people in animal form. The only certain thing is that many people all around the world have seen a phantom black dog in recent times.

Black dog's claw-marks in Blythburgh church.

BIG CATS

THERE MAY BE SOME overlap between phantom black dogs and physical black cats, as the latter are also believed to be present in the UK and someone seeing a large black animal from a distance may not be too sure exactly what it is, nor whether or not it is solid. (Ghostly animals – and people – usually look solid until the witness tries to touch them, or they disappear.) Big cats of all kinds have been reported throughout the UK and it seems undisputable that they are successfully living in the wild, and probably breeding. This is not as alarming as it sounds, for, unless they are startled or threatened, these big cats are secretive animals that like to keep as far away from people as possible.

It is not known when the problem began, but it first came to national awareness during the early 1960s, when the so-called 'Surrey puma' was being widely reported in the Surrey/ Hampshire area of southern England. More recently, the focus of attention has been on southwest England, where, in the 1980s, the 'Exmoor Beast' was being sought. Plenty of evidence has been found to confirm the presence of big cats – footprints, sheep and lambs killed in the way cats are known to kill their prey – and even samples of hair and faeces have been obtained. However, in southwest England, the animals have so far resisted capture, despite efforts using baited cages, and no one has got close enough to shoot one.

Both sandy-coloured and black animals have been seen: the cat below that was photographed on Exmoor by Trevor Beer in 1987 was black.

THE COLOUR OF the cat below, photographed at Morvah in west Cornwall by Selwyn Jolly in 1988, was indeterminate. As the two photographs on these pages show, it is very difficult to get close enough to a big cat to obtain a meaningful photograph which shows any detail. This can only be achieved with dead specimens, as the two photographs overleaf demonstrate.

THIS STUFFED BLACK cat (above) was shot at Kellas in Moray, Scotland, in 1983, after many sightings of big black cats in the area; in fact several were killed there during 1983–85. Although there was speculation that these cats would prove to be a species new to science, analysis has shown that they are complex hybrids of domestic cats and Scottish wildcats. The big cats roaming wild in other parts of the UK still await identification.

SOME UNUSUAL CATS have been found dead after road accidents, such as the jungle cat (opposite). This cat had been seen roaming around Ludlow, Shropshire, UK in 1988. Witnesses described a lynx-like animal and were not believed. When the corpse was obtained, it was identified as an Asian jungle cat, and it had probably either escaped from captivity or been intentionally released. Cryptozoologists continue to hope that an entirely new species of cat will be identified in the UK.

MAN-BEASTS WORLD-WIDE

YETI

BIG HAIRY MONSTERS have been seen in many parts of the world and have been given a variety of names, one book having a nine-page list of them! The best-known is the 'Yeti' or 'Abominable Snowman' (see below), a mysterious creature said to live in the Himalayas of Nepal. There have been many sightings by explorers of strange footprints in the snow, but fewer sightings of the creature itself. One nocturnal visitor stole a carton containing 36 chocolate bars from the camp-site of two mountaineers, and left 12in (30cm) foot-prints leading to and from the tent. It seems to have known what it was looking for, because the bars were wrapped in plastic and packed in a rucksack, and the creature took nothing else. Another pair of mountaineers had lost chocolate bars in similar circumstances on a neighbouring mountain the year before. Who or what could be living at a height of 17,000ft (5,180m) in a night-time temperature of 18 degrees below zero?

Evidence from sherpas and others who claim to have seen the Yeti suggests that it is 7–7½ft (2.1–2.3m) tall, covered with dark brown hair, and has long arms, an oval, pointed head, an ape-like face and less hair on the head and face. It lives in thick forest on the moun-tain slopes, spending the daytime asleep and moving around at night. It comes out onto the snowfields in search of a special moss or lichen rich in vitamins. When out on the snow, it walks upright, but normally it runs on all fours or swings through the trees. In 1970 the British mountaineer Don Whillans briefly saw what may have been a Yeti. By moonlight, and with the aid of binoculars, he watched a black, ape-like shape pulling at snow-covered tree branches. After 20 minutes it made off at speed. Whillans also found human-sized footprints in the snow. There may be more than one kind of creature giving rise to Yeti reports, and cryptozoologists have suggested some possibilities, including an unknown species of anthropoid ape, mountain gorilla, orang-utan, or even some kind of surviving *Gigantopithecus*, a prehis-toric ape-man whose remains have been found in China.

This drawing of a Yeti (left) is by Ivan T. Sanderson, author of *Abominable Snowmen: Legend Come to Life* (1961).

ALMAS

EVERYONE KNOWS ABOUT the Yeti, which is believed to live in the Himalayas, but less well known are the other man-beasts of the remote but vast stretches of country which extend across the former USSR to Mongolia and China. In a Tibetan book describing the wildlife of Mongolia, published in the eighteenth century, is a drawing of a two-legged, hairy creature standing erect on a rock and captioned in three languages (Tibetan, Chinese and Mongolian) as 'man-animal' or 'wildman'. Belief in the existence of the Almas, as the Mongolian man-beast is known, is still widespread today, but opinion is divided as to whether it is merely a myth or a living creature. From time to time expeditions set off into the mountains in search of the Almases, and local people often report sightings. They are said to prefer to live well away from humans and, although apparently fearsome in appearance, with their hair-covered bodies, prominent brows and jaws, stooping gait and long arms, they do not seem to be aggressive towards humans; rather they are suspicious of them. Some researchers believe that the Almas may be a survival of Neanderthal man.

Further west, sightings have been reported from many areas of the southern former USSR, through the Pamir Mountains, Kazakhstan, Tajikistan and Uzbekistan, as far as the Caucasus Mountains between the Caspian and Black Seas. In the Pamirs, the creature is known as Dev, in the Caucasus the name is Kaptar; more than 50 names are known from the former USSR and Mongolia, many of them not easily pronounced, such as Hü Har Göröös (black man-beast). Expeditions regularly visit these areas in search of man-beasts and numerous sighting reports are obtained. Sometimes footprints are found, as shown in the photograph below of investigator Igor Bourtsev holding a cast of a footprint found in the Pamir-Alai Mountains in Tajikistan on 21 August 1979. The print was 13in (33cm) long and 6in (15cm) wide at the toes.

MAN-BEAST CAPTURED

Although many sightings of man-beasts have been reported, and even a few capture attempts made, the most dramatic must surely be the experience recorded by Lt-Col. V. S. Karapetyan, who was able to examine a captured Almas in 1941 a drawing of which appears below. His report is worth quoting in full.

From October to December of 1941 our infantry battalion was stationed some thirty kilometres [18 miles] from the town of Buinaksk [Dagestan]. One day the representatives of the local authorities asked me to examine a man caught in the surrounding mountains and brought to the district centre. My medical advice was needed to establish whether or not this curious creature was a disguised spy.

I entered a shed with two members of the local authorities. When I asked why I had to examine the man in a cold shed and not in a warm room, I was told that the prisoner could not be kept in a warm room. He had sweated in the house so profusely that they had had to keep him in the shed.

I can still see the creature as it stood before me, a male, naked and bare-footed. And it was doubtlessly a man, because its entire shape was human. The chest, back and shoulders, however, were covered with shaggy hair of a dark brown colour. This fur of his was much like that of a bear, and 2 to 3 centimetres [about 1 inch] long. The fur was thinner and softer below the chest. His wrists were crude and sparsely covered with hair. The palms of his hands and soles of his feet were free of hair. But the hair on his head reached to his shoulders, partly covering his forehead. The hair on his head, moreover, felt very rough to the hand. He had no beard or moustache, though his face was completely covered with a light growth of hair. The hair around his mouth was also short and sparse.

The man stood absolutely straight with his arms hanging, and his height was above the average – about 180 cm [6ft]. He stood before me like a giant, his mighty chest thrust forward. His fingers were thick, strong, and exceptionally large. On the whole, he was considerably bigger than any of the local inhabitants.

His eyes told me nothing. They were dull and empty – the eyes of an animal. And he seemed to me like an animal and nothing more.

As I learned, he had accepted no food or drink since he was caught. He had asked for nothing and said nothing. When kept in a warm room he sweated profusely. While I was there, some water and then some food was brought up to his mouth; and someone offered him a hand, but there was no reaction. I gave the verbal conclusion that this was no disguised person, but a wild man of some kind. Then I returned to my unit and never heard of him again. [Karapetyan did learn many years later that the wild-man had been shot.]

Only a few years afterwards, another Almas was trapped in a mountain cabin. It ran on all fours, only standing upright when it was still. The man who cornered it latched the door and went to get a rope, thinking that the creature would be unable to open the door, but when he returned the cabin was empty.

DE LOYS' APE

This photograph was taken by Dr Francis de Loys in 1920, somewhere on the Venezuela–Colombia border in South America.

THE HEAVILY POPULATED areas of the world seem to be the only ones from which no reports of man-beasts have come. Western Europe is presumed to be a man-beast-free zone, but further east, as described earlier (p.41), there are many reported sightings. Even in the northern wasteland of Siberia they have been seen, especially in the eastern area of Yakutia, where they are known as Chuchunaa. Reports have also come from China and throughout South-East Asia, from Australia (the Yowie), from Africa, from South and Central America – but no photographs have ever been obtained that can be considered at all reliable. In this photograph the dead ape-like creature, propped up with a stick, looks intriguing. Dr Francis de Loys was on an expedition in the rainforest in 1920 when two ape-like creatures stepped out of the bushes, walking on their hind legs. They were about 5ft (1.5m) tall and angry, so the party of geologists shot at them, killing the female. Only one of the photographs they took of it survived and this has been the centre of a controversy among cryptozoologists. Some believe it to show a spider monkey, although a larger version than usually seen in the area; others consider it may be an unknown ape, and French zoologist George Montandon gave it the name of *Ameranthropoides loysi* (Loys' American ape). Perhaps the creature is responsible for the reports of ape-men walking upright which have come from places such as Guyana and Nicaragua.

BIGFOOT OR SASQUATCH

IN NORTH AMERICA, there have been over 1,000 reported sightings of the man-beast known as Bigfoot or Sasquatch during the last 150 years, and several thousands more sightings of giant footprints. Despite all this evidence, according to science the creature does not exist because, so far, no corpse has been obtained. According to the reports Bigfoot is usually between 6 and 8ft (1.8 and 2.4m) tall, although some reports have said 10, 12, or even 14ft (3, 3.6 or 4.3m) tall. It walks upright like a man, leaving giant, human-like footprints, and is covered in dark hair. The head hair is often longer than the body hair. The face is flat and usually the creature has no neck.

In 1955 William Roe was able to watch a female Bigfoot eating leaves. He was on a mountain in British Columbia, Canada, when he saw what he at first thought was a grizzly bear – but as it stepped into a clearing he realized that it was certainly not a bear. The 6ft (1.8m) tall creature, with dark brown, silver-tipped hair, was a female with breasts and she weighed around 300lb (136kg). Hidden in a bush, Roe watched as she squatted down 20ft (6m) away and began to strip leaves from a bush with her white, even teeth. He studied her closely and later wrote a detailed description. Eventually she caught his scent and stared directly back at him with an amazed look on her face. She did not attack, but instead walked quickly away. Roe raised his rifle but found he could not bring himself to shoot her, feeling that she was a human being of some kind. This has been the reaction of other witnesses, all of them hunters who know what bears look like and would be able to recognize them easily.

Despite the huge number of sighting reports, genuine photographs of Bigfoot are rare. Most of the known photographs either look like fakes or have dubious origins. The most famous photographs purporting to show Bigfoot are the stills from 30ft (9m) of 16mm colour film, shot on 20 October 1967 by Roger Patterson at Bluff Creek in northern California, USA. Patterson and his friend Bob Gimlin, who had both been searching for Bigfoot for several years and had on a number of occasions made plaster casts of very large footprints, were on horseback, riding through very wild country some 25 miles (40km) from the nearest made-up road. Bigfoot were believed to inhabit this area and so it seemed to be a good place to look out for them. As they rounded a bend, they saw a Bigfoot squatting beside the creek. At that moment their horses saw it too and reared in fright. Patterson's horse fell and he scrambled clear and wrenched his movie camera out of the saddlebag. The creature watched them for a moment and then walked unhurriedly away. Patterson ran after it, trying to get closer and filming at the same time, stumbling and losing his footing as he crossed the shallow creek. He was 80ft (25m) away when he stopped and obtained reasonably clear pictures as the creature took nine paces before becoming partially hidden by trees. Just before this point, and without pausing, it turned to look at the photographer, and large, pendulous, hair-covered breasts are discernible on the movie image, identifying the Bigfoot as a female. Beyond the trees it was much further away and in his excitement Patterson was not holding the camera rock-steady, so there is a certain amount of blur on all the film.

Later the two men took casts of the footprints

Right: A still from Patterson's film, in which the creature's breasts can be seen.

Above: An artist's enhancement of the creature's head.

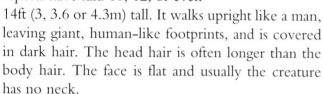

which the creature had made and they were found to measure 14½in (36cm) long by 5½in (14cm) wide.

Inevitably this film is controversial. The two camps are ranged at opposite ends of the argument: those who believe the film to show a genuine Bigfoot, and those who are convinced that it is a man in an ape-suit. There are arguments to support both possibilities, but conclusive proof for neither. It could have been a hoax that fooled Patterson and Gimlin, or they could have been part of a hoax themselves. But Patterson never confessed before he died, and Gimlin has never confessed either.

In the 30 years since Patterson obtained his tantalizing film, many more people have claimed sightings of Bigfoot, and a few have also claimed to have photographed it.

Left: This photograph, showing a normal man's foot alongside one of the footprint casts from the Bigfoot filmed by Roger Patterson, makes clear how big this man-beast really is.

Below: A photograph of Roger Patterson holding casts from the Bigfoot's footprints just a few hours after filming the creature.

THE PHOTOGRAPH BELOW shows a creature with massive shoulders and a relatively small head, allegedly photographed on 11 July 1995 by a forest patrol officer at Wild Creek in the Mount Rainier foothills of Washington State, USA. He was hiking along a ridge when he heard splashing noises and from a high bank he looked down into a swampy lagoon where, 25–30yd (23–27m) away, stood something very large and hairy. He managed to shoot 14 photographs, but because of the light conditions some of them were dark, and this is probably the best one. As always, there are some question-marks over this event: the Bigfoot seems strangely motionless from shot to shot; its head seems unnaturally small and pushed into its shoulders; the photographer is conveniently anonymous, and seems to have been unusually brave, for few people would have stayed long enough to take 14 photographs with such a monster close at hand. Many researchers believe these photographs to be hoaxes.

Until someone finds a Bigfoot carcase, or a Bigfoot is deliberately shot, these photographs are the best evidence we have for the creature's existence and, as we have seen, they are really no better than no evidence at all!

MINNESOTA ICEMAN

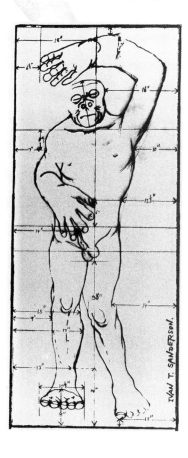

IN 1968 SOME people believed that a genuine corpse of a man-beast had been found and was being kept frozen in a block of ice in Minnesota, USA. It was being used as a money-earning attraction and was carted around to different locations as a side-show. In December 1968 cryptozoologists Ivan T. Sanderson and Dr Bernard Heuvelmans went to Minnesota to see it and, despite the problems of conducting an examination of something that was frozen into a semi-opaque block of ice, they agreed that it appeared to be the fresh corpse of a hitherto unknown form of living hominid. However, the truth will probably never be known, for it was said that the owner of the corpse later substituted a model. Whether this is what really happened, or whether there never was a real corpse, is likely to remain a mystery. The picture below shows part of the corpse (or model) while the drawings (left and right) were made by Ivan Sanderson after seeing what he believed was a genuine corpse.

Fig. 1 Scale drawing of the specimen.

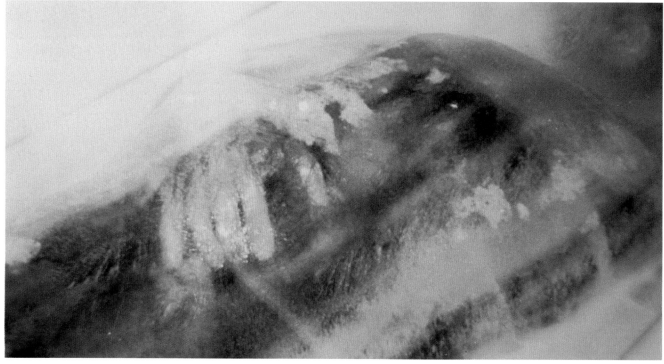

ANIMAL MYSTERIES

WINGED CATS

NATURE IS OVERFLOWING with mysteries, one of which is cats that seem to have wings. From time to time, cats have been found that have fur-covered extensions on their backs, looking just like wings. A cat called Thomas Bessie was exhibited as a side-show in a fairground in 1900, until he died suddenly, possibly of poisoning. His 'wings' were said to be malformations of the rib structure. The Oxford winged cat of the 1930s was said to be able to fly, using his wings like a bird. However, the 2ft (60cm) wingspan of Sally, another cat from the 1930s, did not enable her to fly.

About 20 years ago, a winged cat made its home in a builder's yard in Manchester, UK, having strayed there as a kitten. The 'wings', which developed as the cat grew, were about 11in (29cm) from the shoulder-bone to the wingtip, and the cat also had an unusual tail, broad and flat. The photograph on the left shows that the 'wings' were very definite furry extensions, but maybe they were nothing more than matted fur, as sometimes happens to long-haired cats. Alternatively, the animal may have had a rare skin disorder, called feline cutaneous asthenia (FCA), which makes the skin very elastic, especially on the back and shoulders. It might be possible in such a case for long extensions of skin to develop, covered with fur and incorporating muscle fibres which could account for them being moved like flapping wings. Such projections are known to peel off easily without bleeding, which could explain the winged cats whose wings have suddenly dropped off. The photograph below shows a winged cat at Wiveliscombe, Somerset, UK, in 1899.

RAT KINGS

THE SO-CALLED 'rat king' presents an as-yet-unsolved mystery: why do the tails of a group of rats sometimes become inextricably intertwined? Although rare, this phenomenon is well documented. The rat king shown in the photograph was X-rayed and the result showed that the tails were indeed knotted together, and that there were some tail fractures as a result. Callus formation showed that the knotting had not happened immediately before death, so does that mean that the rats suffered a lingering death? There seems no way they could have obtained food in that condition. No one knows how or why rat kings form, although it might happen when a group of rats huddle together for warmth. Similar 'kings' of mice and squirrels have been found, and also of kittens born with their umbilical cords intertwined.

The two rat kings illustrated both came from Germany. One (shown in the engraving above) was discovered by a German miller when it fell out of his machinery in 1748 – the animals were still alive. The other (see the photograph below), now in the Göttingen Zoological Museum, was found in Ruderhausen, near the Harz Mountains, in 1907. The most recent example we know of was found by a Dutch farmer in his barn in 1963.

JERSEY DEVIL

IN JANUARY 1909, the State of New Jersey in the USA was visited by a very weird 'winged thing', which became known as the Jersey Devil. One of the earliest witnesses was E. W. Minster, the Postmaster of Bristol, Pennsylvania, USA, just over the border from New Jersey.

> I awoke about two o'clock in the morning . . . and finding myself unable to sleep, I arose and wet my head with cold water as a cure for insomnia.
>
> As I got up I heard an eerie, almost super-natural sound from the direction of the river . . . I looked out upon the Delaware and saw flying diagonally across what appeared to be a large crane, but which was emitting a glow like a fire-fly.
>
> Its head resembled that of a ram, with curled horns, and its long thick neck was thrust forward in flight. It had long thin wings and short legs, the front legs shorter than the hind. Again, it uttered its mournful and awful call – a combination of a squawk and a whistle, the beginning very high and piercing and ending very low and hoarse.

Two days later, in Gloucester City, New Jersey, Mr and Mrs Nelson Evans watched the monster (see the drawing below) for ten minutes on their shed roof at 2 a.m., and described it as:

> . . . about three and a half feet high [0.9–1m], with a head like a collie dog and a face like a horse. It had a long neck, wings about two feet [60cm] long, and its back legs were like those of a crane, and it had horse's hooves. It walked on its back legs and held up two short front legs with paws on them. It didn't use the front legs at all while we were watching. My wife and I were scared, I tell you, but I managed to open the window and say, 'Shoo!', and it turned around, barked at me, and flew away.

The Evanses referred to the creature's feet as being like horse's hooves and, indeed, people reported finding its footprints (shown in the photograph). Numerous sightings of the Jersey Devil were made during that amazing week of 16–23 January 1909; then the mystery creature disappeared as suddenly as it had appeared.

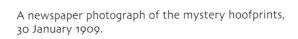

A newspaper photograph of the mystery hoofprints, 30 January 1909.

CATTLE MUTILATION

OVER THE LAST 25 years or so, there have been many reported cases in the USA of so-called 'cattle mutilation': cattle found dead of unknown causes, often mutilated with apparently surgical precision, their blood often drained, and certain organs (especially the reproductive organs) removed. The killings usually occur in isolated areas far from roads, and no footprints are left. Sceptics believe that the usual predators are at work, but so far no culprit has been identified, although many people believe that UFOs and aliens are somehow involved. The photograph shows a mutilated animal in New Mexico being examined by State Police Officer Gabe Valdez who, in the 1970s, co-ordinated interstate investigation of livestock mutilations.

TOADS IN STONES

ANOTHER UNSOLVED MYSTERY of the animal kingdom is that of toads found inside stones. The toads have usually been found by quarry workmen, who have seen them emerging from stones that have been smashed open. The earliest British report we have found dates back to the seventeenth century when Dr Richard Richardson described how he saw workmen break open a stone:

> wherein was contained a toad . . . which, being laid upon the ground, crawled about as long as the sun shone warm upon it, but towards night died.

Toads have been found in all kinds of rock and, in 1910, someone in Leicestershire discovered one while breaking open a lump of coal:

> . . . from the centre a live half-grown toad fell out on its back. I called the attention of my neighbours to it, and I thought it was dead: but in a few minutes it began to move about . . .

Only a few years later, in 1919, a miner working about 200yd (180m) underground in a Derbyshire colliery found a 3in (7.5cm) live toad, dirty brown in colour, in a pocket in the coal:

> Its eyes were open, but it was obvious that it could not see at first. Two days afterwards, it gave indications of returning to normal. The toad has no mouth, but there are evidences that it once possessed this useful member. On the same day as the sight began to return the toad started to leap about in a clumsy manner. The webbed feet differ from the present well-known varieties.

Toads and frogs are still being found: in 1982 workmen laying a railway culvert in New Zealand found two live frogs sealed under 12ft (3.6m) of rock. The unanswerable question is: have these frogs and toads been incarcerated during the millions of years since their muddy world solidified into rock? It seems impossible, and yet . . .

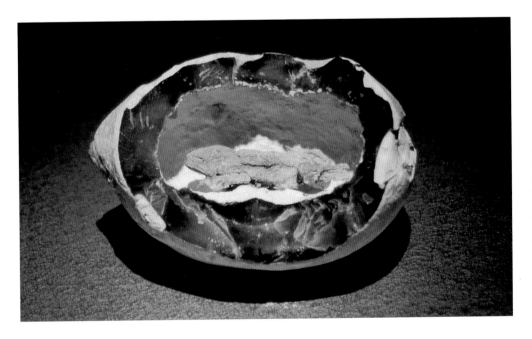

This example was discovered early this century, in 1901, inside a flint nodule that was cracked open by workmen in a quarry near Lewes, Sussex, UK. It was, however, mummified. It can still be seen in the Booth Museum in Brighton, to which it was given by Charles Dawson (who was a known hoaxer, and therefore there must be some uncertainty as to the authenticity of this example).

GHOSTS
AND SPIRITS

INTRODUCTION

GHOSTS HAVE ALWAYS been with us and are as much of a mystery now as they were in the first century AD, when Athenodorus, a hard-up philosopher, rented a house in Athens, which was cheap because of its eerie reputation. It lived up to this reputation on the very first night he was there. Sitting working late at night, Athenodorus heard the rattling of chains and then, suddenly, the horrifying figure of an old man appeared before him. It beckoned to him and, although Athenodorus tried to ignore it and get on with his work, it refused to let him, rattling its chains so that he couldn't concentrate. So Athenodorus followed the ghost into the garden, where it pointed at a spot on the ground and disappeared. Next day, a hole was dug at the place indicated by the ghost and a human skeleton with chains still around it was discovered. After the remains were given a proper burial and the house purified, the haunting ceased.

This was clearly a ghost with a purpose, but usually the reason for a haunting is not clear. There have been a few modern cases where ghosts seemed to have a message, such as 'crisis apparitions' of a person, seen by close friends and relatives at the time of his/her death, an event unknown to them until comfirmation came later. However, in many ghost sightings, the apparition seems purposeless and its identity remains unknown.

Some people are sceptical and do not believe in the existence of ghosts. It is indeed likely that some witnesses who claim to have seen ghosts out of doors have, in fact, mistaken a swirling patch of mist for a human figure, especially if they have been alone and the place was eerie. Other people may have vivid imaginations and 'see' externally something that is really only in their mind. However, considering how long the concept of ghosts and hauntings has been in existence, it is unlikely that all the reports result from imagination, misidentification or down-right hoaxing. Also, this is a mystery which is supported by photographs. Since the invention of photography over a century ago, people have been capturing ghosts on film. Of course such photographs can be a hoax – two examples of such ghost photographs are shown on p.63 – but to dismiss all the photographs reproduced here as hoaxes would be a dangerous denial of a genuine mystery.

Another genuine mystery is to be found in the persistent reports of poltergeist phenomena. The poltergeist (see p.79) can be responsible for creating fear and chaos in households, throwing objects around, making things disappear and reappear, producing puddles of water and so on. When fire-raising is added to this repertoire, the experience becomes truly frightening. In 1922, a lonely farm-house in Nova Scotia, Canada, was the location for some weird events. One night in January, between 5 p.m. and 8 a.m., 38 separate fires broke out and were extinguished by the old man who lived there with his wife and their 15-year-old adopted daughter. A neighbour, who was an electrician, was puzzled by what he saw, including a pale blue flame that was not hot and a blaze breaking out on wet wallpaper. The next night 31 fires broke out and even though the house was wet through from water used to put out the fires, they still kept flaring up. One fire-fighter picked up a piece of wet paper and a water-soaked rag, both of which burst into flame. The teenage girl was thought by some to be responsible, but it is unlikely that she started the fires deliberately. The pent-up energy and frustration of the growing youngster may somehow express themselves in para-normal happenings of this kind, but as yet the force behind poltergeist events of any kind, including spontaneous fires, has not been identified.

In some poltergeist cases, an invisible entity claims to be responsible, although a figure is rarely seen. However, on rare occasions, a poltergeist will speak. This happened in the Enfield case in the UK in recent years (see p.79), and also in an earlier case, again in Canada. The location of the latter was the village of Clarendon, in Quebec Province, and the year was 1889. The focus seemed to be an 11-year-old Scottish girl, Dinah McLean, who had recently been adopted from an orphanage. The newly built, single-storey log house where she lived was plagued with all manner of unpleasant events, including excreta from the outdoor toilet being brought indoors and placed in the food

cupboard and in the food, beds and other places. Windows were smashed and spontaneous fires broke out. Dinah's pigtail was roughly cut, as if by a knife, and then she began to see things: a big black shape pulling off the bedclothes. Dinah hit it with a whip and everyone present heard a noise like a pig squealing. Then the daughter of the family, four-year-old Mary, claimed to see a man with the head, horns and feet of a cow standing at the front door and later she saw him putting sugar into the oven. The figure turned to her and said: 'Little girl, would you like to go to hell with me?' Dinah heard a gruff voice talking to her, uttering obscenities. Gradually the plump, rosy-cheeked girl grew thin, with dark rings around her eyes.

Next the voice began to speak to other people, including Percy Woodcock, a distinguished artist with an interest in the paranormal who had gone to Clarendon to investigate the poltergeist. On hearing a gruff voice speaking obscenely to him, Woodcock asked: 'Who are you?' The voice replied: 'I am the Devil. I'll have you in my clutches. Get out of this or I'll break your neck.' To make sure he was not being tricked, Woodcock asked Dinah to go and fill her mouth with water. She did so, but the voice kept on talking. Woodcock asked the voice to write something and saw a pencil lift itself off the bench and begin to write on the paper that was set out. It wrote obscenities and, when Woodcock complained, the voice threatened to steal the pencil, which then flew through the air. Events became

even more bizarre when the voice claimed a change of identity; it was now an angel, and joined in with several hours of hymn-singing performed by a crowd that had gathered, now having a voice of 'sweetness and light'. It finally took its leave in the early hours of the morning, appearing briefly one last time on the following morning, when the three children at the house claimed to have seen the ghost looking like an angel, complete with gold crown and stars.

Perhaps it is also angels – or rather, dead people who have gone to join the angels – that appear on 'spirit photographs'. Spirit photography was very popular during the late nineteenth and early twentieth centuries and, as the photographs show, some intriguing portraits of identifiable dead people floating in the air behind the portraits of the living were obtained. Unfortunately, some of the mediums who produced these pictures were found to be cheating by substituting photographic glass plates (which were used at that time instead of film) onto which the faces had already been imprinted. Nevertheless, there are still some unusual photographs which, it is claimed, were taken in circumstances where fraud was not possible. At this same time, many mediums were claiming the ability to produce a mysterious substance, known as 'ectoplasm', which could form itself into the faces of the dead. Some mediums also claimed to be able to materialize a spirit form, which sitters could touch as it walked among them, although usually in a darkened room. Sometimes mediums would allow photographs to be taken, some of which appear in this section. These claims were investigated at the time, although often by people inclined to belief in them, so their reports cannot be considered objective and reliable. Even though the materialization mediums have gone, the core phenomena of ghosts and poltergeists continue to be experienced. Such events have been investigated impartially, yet they still defy explanation.

GHOSTS IN PHOTOGRAPHS

DOES THIS PHOTOGRAPH show the Black Abbot, a hooded figure in a black cloak who is said to walk through Prestbury churchyard near Cheltenham, Gloucestershire, UK? The figure was not seen at the time by the photographer, Derek Stafford, who was in the churchyard on the night of 22 November 1990, taking photographs of the floodlit gravestones. The ghostly figure showed up on his very last photograph when the film was developed.

IN 1677 THE small market town of Wem in north Shropshire, UK, was devastated by a fire which, so it was said, was started accidentally by a young girl. She knocked over a lighted candle which set fire to the thatched roof of the cottage where she lived, and this fire then spread rapidly through the town. Now, over 300 years later, she may have returned, drawn back to the scene of the earlier disaster by another major fire in the town.

It was on 19 November 1995 that the town hall at Wem was destroyed by fire, an event watched from a safe distance by Tony O'Rahilly, a local amateur photographer. He took some photographs of the blaze, which he later developed at home, and when he printed them he was surprised to see the figure of what appears to be a young girl in one of the pictures, shown below (the inset shows the girl close up). She is standing in the doorway of the fire escape, surrounded by smoke and flames. No living person could have been standing there, because it was too dangerous, and the fire-fighters were keeping people away. She appears to have long hair, and to be wearing an old-fashioned bonnet. However she may not be the girl from the seventeenth century. Another theory supposes that she is a dead actress who has come back to the place where she acted in amateur dramatics earlier this century.

Not everyone has accepted that the photograph shows a ghost. The photographer has been accused of hoaxing it, although there is no evidence for this, and he is adamant that the photograph is genuine. Other doubters have explained it as a coincidence, with the burning timbers just happening to look like a girl's face, but it is interesting that workmen who were working in the town hall after the fire claimed to have seen a ghost there. So it seems that this strange photograph cannot be easily dismissed.

Professional photographer Haddon Davies was undertaking a routine assignment on 22 January 1985 when he went to the medieval St Mary's Guildhall in Coventry, in the English Midlands, to photograph the Coventry Freeman's Guild dinner. He climbed up into the ancient minstrels' gallery and set up his tripod and camera among the suits of armour, swords and pikestaffs. A ten-second exposure was necessary because of the dim lighting in the large hall, so Mr Davies waited until everyone was standing up to say grace before he took his photograph. Later, when an enlargement was made for the Lord Mayor, people who looked at it noticed a strange figure at the end of the top table (see the photograph and close-up below). Despite much discussion, no one could offer any logical explanation for the figure, which looked as if it might be wearing some sort of medieval costume or armour. Mr Davies checked the test photographs he had made both before and after the chosen picture, but the strange figure was nowhere to be seen. The Lord Mayor had a guest list and was able to account for everyone except the enigmatic visitor, and the people sitting in that area had no recollection of seeing the strange figure.

Some of the staff at the fourteenth-century hall were not surprised by the suggestion that the building might be haunted and, as Mr Davies commented: 'It seems that, just as I had felt, the hall was no place in which to work alone after dark.' One of the few historic buildings in Coventry to survive World War Two unscathed, the Guildhall stands next door to the site of the cathedral, which was demolished by the war-time bombing. The hall was built in 1340–42 and enlarged c.1400, and the tapestry which can be seen in the photograph is about 500 years old. Was the ghostly figure a participant in some historic event there, brought back to fleeting 'life' by the disassociated mental energy of the assembled company as they all stood quietly?

EXCEPT FOR THE ghost on the staircase in Raynham Hall (see p.64), all the photographs in this section have one thing in common: the photographer never saw the ghost when he was taking the photograph. There are two possible conclusions to draw from this: either there is some other straightforward explanation for the 'ghost', or photographic film can capture things which are present but not visible to the human eye. Often it is just not possible to decide which is the correct explanation. The figure seen here in the cellar of the Viaduct Inn in London, UK, where the cells of Newgate Prison were said to have stood, looks real enough but Lars Thomas, the photographer, is sure that there was no one standing in front of him at the time. In 1988 Lars was on a guided tour of the cellar and wanted to capture the eerie place on film, so he made sure his picture was not going to show any of the other visitors. As he is a friend of ours, we know that he is not the sort of person to make a mistake. So who is this ghostly figure?

THE PHOTOGRAPH SHOWN on the left bears some similarity to the one taken in the cellar of the Viaduct Inn, because the photographer, Eddie Coxon, made sure that there was no one in front of the camera before taking it. He was photographing the interior of Alton church in Staffordshire, UK, during a flower festival on 12 September 1993. He made a 2–3 second exposure and did not use any flash. The resulting photograph seems to show blurred figures, but insufficient detail makes any identification impossible.

IN 1991, WHEN he was two years old, Greg Sheldon Maxwell started saying 'Old Nanna's here!', while pointing up into the air. He was referring to his late great-grandmother, who used to say to her daughter that she wanted her to see her when she was dead. When this photograph (right) was taken, nobody saw anything unusual, but Greg certainly seems to be looking at something. Was he seeing Old Nanna in the mist?

Two years later, when Greg and his mother were in England for a few months (the family normally lived in Abu Dhabi), and visiting his grandmother, he was asked if he still saw Old Nanna. He said 'No, but I can show you what she looks like' and took his mother and grandmother into the hall at his grandmother's home. He pointed to a photograph on the wall and said: 'That's how she looked when I saw her.' He had never mentioned the photograph before and presumably hadn't been told who was depicted in it.

HOAXES

Do these ghosts look genuine? In fact they are easily made fakes which anyone can set up. Just drape a friend in an old white sheet and fix your camera on a tripod. Photograph the scene, then wind the film back, being careful not to move the camera. Position the 'ghost' within the scene and then rephotograph it. If you try this and get good results, one thing you must never do is pretend it is a real ghost. There are too many hoaxers in the world already! This light-hearted exercise in ghost photography holds a serious message: you should never take anything for granted. Just because someone says a photograph shows a ghost is no guarantee that it really does. You need to make enquiries and to check the circumstances of the event and the veracity of the photographer before deciding whether the photograph could be genuine. However, this doesn't mean you should reject such pictures dogmatically. There must be nothing more frustrating for someone who has obtained a genuinely mysterious photograph, be it of a ghost, a UFO, a lake monster or whatever, than to find nobody believes you!

HOAX OR GENUINE?

AYNHAM HALL IS a seventeenth-century mansion in Norfolk, UK, said to be haunted by the Brown Lady. She was thought to be the ghost of Dorothy Walpole, who became Lady Townshend. The ghost was known as the Brown Lady because, in her portrait, Lady Dorothy wore a brown dress. She was often seen in past centuries and, on one occasion, the popular novelist Captain Marryat fired his pistol at her. The ghost disappeared and the bullet was found lodged in the door behind where she had stood. She was also seen by King George IV (then Regent) when he was staying at the hall in the early nineteenth century. He awoke to find a pale-faced woman with untidy hair and a brown dress standing by the bed. Another witness, Colonel Loftus, who saw her on two successive nights in 1835, said there were dark hollows where her eyes should have been.

In 1936 she was captured on film by two photographers working at the hall. They had taken a number of pictures when they came to the staircase. Then, as Indra Shira later wrote:

> Captain Provand took one photograph while I flashed the light. He was focusing for another exposure: I was standing by his side just behind the camera with the flashlight pistol in my hand, looking directly up the staircase. All at once I detected an ethereal veiled form coming slowly down the stairs. Rather excitedly I called out sharply: 'Quick, quick, there's something.' I pressed the trigger of the flashlight pistol. After the flash and on closing the shutter, Captain Provand removed the focusing cloth from his head, and turning to me said: 'What's all the excitement about?'

The Captain, on being told that there had been a ghost on the stair, offered to bet £5 that there would be nothing on the negative. The two men argued all the way back to London, and asked a friend to watch while the film was developed. They were adamant that the negative had not been interfered with in any way and that they had genuinely photographed a ghost. Perhaps she put in an appearance at that time, when she knew there were photographers in the hall, in an attempt to prove that ghosts do exist!

THERE IS AN old church to be found in most English villages and many of these buildings are of great historical interest, some of them being almost 1,000 years old. It is hardly surprising, therefore, that many of them are also said to be haunted. Ghostly clergymen have been seen, and ghostly monks, as well as white ladies, knights dressed in armour and children. Some people have smelled incense; others have heard ghostly voices singing or the organ mysteriously playing, but the figure who appeared on a photograph of Newby church has never been seen by anyone!

Newby church is in North Yorkshire, in the north of England, and 30 years ago the priest in charge there was the Reverend K. F. Lord. He was a keen amateur photographer and one summer afternoon in the early 1960s he decided to photograph the inside of the church. There was no one else there with him except a friend. Some time later, when he made some prints from the negatives, he discovered the ghost on one of them. Standing beside the altar is a tall, menacing figure, wrapped in a long, dark cloak. Its face seems to be covered by a white cloth with eye-holes. Until this photograph was taken, the church was not known to be haunted and the identity of the figure remains a mystery.

IT IS NOT only ghosts of people that can appear in photographs. Ghostly animals have been the subjects of numerous photographs, among them the three shown here.

The photograph (right) shows a garden tea-party at Tingewick, in Buckinghamshire, UK. It was taken *c.*1916 by a retired CID Inspector from Scotland Yard, Arthur Springer. Although a dog can be seen in the left foreground of the picture, he did not see any dog at the time, nor did the people taking tea. It is clearly standing still and therefore, if it had been a live dog, it would have appeared as solid as the people. Instead, it is insubstantial, and appears to be headless.

THIS FAMILY GROUP, with the lady and her two children (right), was photographed at Clarens, in Switzerland, in August 1925. The boy is seen to have a toy animal in his hands, but the tiny head of a white kitten is also visible (see the close-up above), although he was not holding a kitten at the time. It was recognized as a white kitten which had belonged to the family, but which had died some weeks earlier after being mauled by a dog.

THIS PHOTOGRAPH SHOWING Lady Hehir and her wolfhound with an extra head on its rear end, was taken in 1926. The extra head was identified as belonging to a Cairn terrier puppy named Kathal, which had died six weeks before this photograph was taken. Kathal and Tara had both lived with Lady Hehir and she said they had been inseparable, eating, playing and walking together. The place where the photograph was taken had been a favourite spot of theirs.

PHANTOM HITCH-HIKERS

ENGLAND HAS MORE than its fair share of these ghostly would-be travellers and they are definitely not all tall tales. On 12 October 1979, Roy Fulton was going home after a darts match at the pub. He had not had a great deal to drink. As he drove through the village of Stanbridge, near Dunstable in Bedfordshire, he saw a figure standing beside the road thumbing a lift, so he stopped. The man walked towards the van and, in the headlights, Fulton could see that he was wearing dark trousers and jumper and a white, open-necked shirt. The man opened the door and got in, but when Fulton asked where he was going, he did not reply but only pointed along the road. After driving for several minutes in silence, Fulton turned to offer his

All around the world there are stories of ghostly happenings on the roads, usually at night. A car runs into somebody but when the driver gets out, feeling very shocked, he finds that there is no one there. Sometimes the ghost seen on the road is a hitch-hiker, but looks very much alive. The driver stops for him/her, the hitch-hiker gets in — but when they reach the destination, the driver finds that there is no one in the car. Sometimes the tale is more complicated and the hitch-hiker gives an address. The driver calls at the address, only to find that the hitch-hiker has been dead for some years, having been killed in a road accident at the very spot where the driver picked him/her up.

passenger a cigarette and found there was no one beside him. He checked that the man had not climbed over the seat into the back: it was not possible for him to have got out of the van without being noticed.

Roy Fulton (second from right) in his local pub.

Haunted Blue Bell Hill.

EVEN MORE STRANGE were the events of 1958, when a lorry-driver encountered the same hitch-hiker on several different occasions. This happened on a certain stretch of road in Somerset, and the driver began to think there was something odd happening when one night he saw the familiar hitch-hiker waving his torch and stopped for him. The hitch-hiker said he had to fetch some cases but never came back and, after 20 minutes, the lorry-driver decided to leave without him. About 3 miles (5km) along the road the lorry-driver saw him again – but it was impossible for him to have got there, because no traffic had passed the lorry. Now very alarmed, the driver decided not to stop but the man jumped into the path of the lorry and was run over. The driver got out – but there was no corpse, only the hitch-hiker standing in the road shaking his fist. Then he turned away and vanished. Other drivers have also reported seeing a phantom hitch-hiker on the same road in more recent years.

Another location where numerous drivers have reported seeing either phantom accidents or phantom hitch-hikers is Blue Bell Hill near Maidstone, Kent, UK (see the photograph above). Sometimes a ghostly girl waves at a car and asks for a lift. She is said to be a bride-to-be or a bridesmaid, who was killed in a car crash at the bottom of the hill. In July 1974 a man driving on the hill after midnight saw a girl appear in his headlights and the car ran into her. He got out and found a young girl lying on the road, with bleeding head and knees. He carried her to the pavement and wrapped her in a blanket before he drove to the police station for help but, when the police went to the scene, they couldn't find the girl; there was only the blanket she had been wrapped in, and no trace of any blood.

A
T LEAST THREE separate drivers have picked up a phantom hitch-hiker on the same stretch of road near Uniondale in South Africa. One of them was Dawie van Jaarsveld (right), who was riding his motorcycle one night in April 1978 when he saw a girl standing by the road. He offered her a lift but couldn't hear her mumbled reply when he asked where she wanted to be dropped. He gave her a crash helmet to wear, and a transistor radio earplug so she could listen to the music, as he was doing. After 10 miles (16km) he thought his back wheel was skidding and stopped to check his tyre. He was amazed to find his passenger gone. The helmet was strapped to the seat and the earplug was fixed into his other ear, although his crash helmet was firmly in position. He commented: 'I can tell you, the moment I realized these things I could feel the hair stand on end on my head and I had cold shivers up and down my spine.' A researcher we know personally, Cynthia Hind, checked the man's story by visiting the café in Uniondale, where he called immediately after the unnerving experience, and also his girlfriend's home, and everyone confirmed that he had looked as if he had seen a ghost.

It seems that other drivers have had similar experiences. One of them was Anton Le Grange, who picked up the ghost in his car on 12 May 1976. Cynthia Hind spoke to the policeman who saw Le Grange when he came to report the incident, and he confirmed that Le Grange had been deadly serious and had made the policeman go with him to the car, where he saw the door open and close of its own accord. After Le Grange's experience was reported in the press, a pilot came forward and said that his fiancée, Maria Roux, had been killed in a car crash on 12 April 1968 at the spot where the ghost had been seen. Le Grange identified the girl in the photograph as being very like the girl he had picked up, and wearing similar clothes to those Maria was wearing when she died. She seems to appear only around the time she died, and only to single young men. On 4 April 1980, André Coetzee, aged 20, was motorcycling past the accident site when he felt

Dawie van Jaarsveld, who gave a lift to a phantom hitchhiker.

'someone or something put its arms around my waist from behind. There was something sitting on my bike'. The ghost seemed to be annoyed when André speeded up and it hit him on the head. It disappeared when André reached 100 mph (160km/h) and, by the time he stopped at a café, he could hardly speak.

If ghosts really do exist, it is not surprising that so many of them are seen on roads. Sudden and unexpected death in road accidents may be just the kind of crisis event that gives rise to a haunting; it is often the case that a person who reappears as a ghost suffered some traumatic event during life, such as a violent or sudden death.

Maria Roux, who died tragically in 1968.

The road sign is at the Barandas turn-off, where the ghost of the female hitch-hiker has been seen.

HAUNTED PLACES

BORLEY RECTORY

KNOWN AS 'the most haunted house in England', Borley Rectory was a large, rambling house, built in Victorian times for the rector of Borley, a small village in the county of Essex in eastern England. In the 1860s, when it was built, families were larger than they are today and the first rector to live in the rectory, the Reverend Henry D. E. Bull, had 14 children. After Bull's death, his son Harry, who succeeded him as rector, lived there with his brothers and sisters, and it was during this time that ghostly phenomena were first noticed. Four of the sisters saw a phantom nun on the rectory lawn, and she was also seen by other people. More ghosts were seen, as well as a ghostly coach, and poltergeist phenomena were experienced, with objects mysteriously moving about.

Borley Rectory, and the gate where the phantom nun was seen.

After Harry Bull's death in 1927, the rectory stood empty for a year, and then the Reverend and Mrs G. Eric Smith moved in. Perhaps foolishly, they contacted a national newspaper to try and find a psychical research society to investigate the strange happenings. The newspaper editor sent a reporter who was looking for a good story, and he was followed by a publicity-loving researcher, Harry Price. Price heard the Smiths' reports of whisperings and strange voices, of dragging footsteps, bell-ringing and ghosts. Even more things began to happen after Price arrived on the scene: stones and bricks were thrown; a mysterious light was seen in an empty part of the house; there was a sighting of the phantom nun; bells were heard ringing; and there was a shower of keys. Mrs Smith was suspicious and wondered if Price himself might be causing some of the 'mysterious' events.

This photograph, taken in March 1939, shows the ruins of the rectory after it was burnt down.

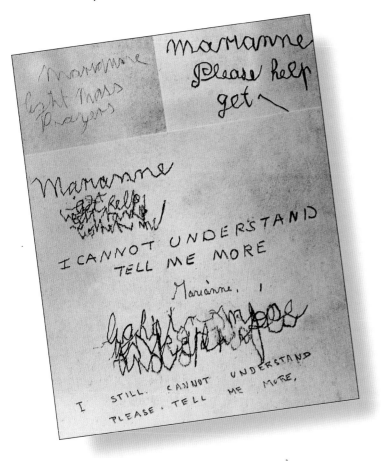

Some of the messages written in pencil on the walls of Borley Rectory; the words in capital letters were written by investigators trying to communicate with the spirit entity.

Disturbed by what was happening, the Smiths left, and the Reverend and Mrs Foyster took up residence in 1930. From this time onward, there was a dramatic increase in the number of strange incidents: voices, footsteps, ghosts, strange smells, movement of objects, bell-ringing, mysterious fires, messages written on the walls and on papers, wine turning into ink, etc. Harry Price believed that the Foysters were responsible for most of what was happening. After they left, he took over the house himself and noted a few ghostly events, such as strange noises, writings on the walls and footsteps. He kept the house for a year and, a few months after he left, it was destroyed by fire.

Even though the house had been reduced to a shell, strange happenings were still reported and, although it has long been demolished and the site built over, there are still reports of ghostly phenomena from the old church across the road.

GHOSTLY ARMIES

MANY BLOODY BATTLES have been fought on Britain's soil during the last 1,000 years, and these battles have shaped the country's history. Being strongly emotional events, with the soldiers experiencing terror as well as unbearable physical pain, it is not surprising that these battles have also left their mark in the form of ghostly events that are still being witnessed several hundred years later.

Probably the best-known haunted battlefield in England is at Edge Hill in Warwickshire, in the Midlands, where the first battle of the Civil War was fought in 1642. The photograph below, taken in winter, shows the battle site from Edge Hill. Two months after the battle, at Christmas-time, some shepherds and travellers were journeying through the darkness when, just after midnight, they heard the sound of drums and soldiers groaning. They thought a battle was taking place all around them in the darkness – until they saw that the activity was happening in the sky! It continued until 2 or 3 o'clock in the morning and the petrified witnesses were too scared to run away, so they watched for three hours, until eventually the phantom battle ended and all the ghosts vanished. People who visited the battlefield the next night were rewarded with another re-run of the battle, as were visitors on subsequent nights. Six of King Charles I's officers also saw the ghostly battle, and some of them claimed to recognize comrades who had been killed in the real battle. Today, people visit the battlefield on the anniversary of the battle, but now the only ghostly phenomena reported are the neighing of invisible horses and strange lights above the fields where the battle was fought.

At other haunted battlefields, only the sounds of battle are heard and nothing is seen. Over 700 years ago, Offham Hill, near Lewes in southern England, was the site of a great battle in which 3,000 men died and, in late May, the time of year when the battle was fought, people have reported hearing strange noises of men shouting and horses whinnying. Similarly, in a village in Norfolk, UK, a couple found themselves in the midst of a phantom battle early one morning when walking home from visiting friends. They heard shouting, running feet and galloping horses, but could see nothing. They felt that they were surrounded by all the noises of a real battle, which gradually moved away into a field.

A lady out late one night in 1950, this time in Scotland, saw some strange events which may have been a ghostly re-enactment of the Battle of Nechtanesmere, which was fought in AD 685, 1,265 years before. Her car had skidded on the icy road and run into the ditch, so she had to leave her vehicle there and walk the rest of the way home through country lanes. She was carrying her small dog and feeling very tired. Suddenly she saw people carrying flaming torches, and the dog obviously saw them too because he began to growl. She saw men turning over bodies on the ground, as if looking for their dead comrades, and when she later described the men's clothing to an historical researcher, her description matched the dress of Pictish warriors carved on ancient stones.

Again in Scotland, on the island of Iona, a ghostly fleet of Viking longboats has been seen more than once. One witness described seeing 14 ships land and the Viking occupants attack and slaughter a group of monks who were standing on shore; they then seized their cattle and possessions from the nearby abbey and set the building alight before sailing out to sea again. These events may originally have taken place in AD 986, when such terrible tragedies were only too familiar. Today most people only see such things in films . . . except when someone happens to step into a time-slip and become, for a few moments, an eyewitness to events of a past long gone.

MARSTON MOOR

Ghosts are sometimes seen at haunted battlefields, for example at Marston Moor in North Yorkshire, where a major battle was fought in 1644. (The photograph shows the battlefield memorial.) People crossing the area at night have seen men in old-fashioned clothing who seem to be the ghosts of soldiers. In 1960, also in northern England, a lady and her taxi-driver saw phantom soldiers at the site of the Battle of Otterburn (1388) in Northumberland. She said: 'Suddenly the engine died, the fare-meter went haywire and the taxi felt as if it was being forced against an invisible wall. The soldiers seemed to close in on us then fade into thin air.' Other people have seen phantom soldiers here and one lady saw them three times!

ONE OF THE most vivid apparitions of soldiers on record was that seen in 1953 by 18-year-old Harry Martindale. An apprentice plumber, Martindale was working at the time in the Treasurer's House in York, UK. One day he was at work in in the cellar, when, to his astonishment and fright he saw a Roman soldier step out of the wall. What he did not know at the time was that his ladder was standing on the course of an old Roman road. He later described in detail what he had witnessed:

I heard a sound – the only way I can describe it is the sound of a musical note. It was just like a trumpet blaring out – no tune, just a blare. At the same time, a figure came out of the wall. And the head of the figure was in line with my waist, with a shining helmet. I knew that it shouldn't be here, and when I say that I was terrified, I mean that I *was* terrified. I fell off the ladder and scrambled into the corner . . . and from there, I got a bird's eye view of what it was. It was the head of a Roman soldier.

The figure crossed the room and disappeared into a pillar. It was followed by another soldier on horseback and then by soldiers walking in pairs, side by side. Martindale continued:

> Now I was in no fit state to count them, but as I say, at the time I took a count of between 12 and 20. I was suffering from severe shock, and the immediate relief I got was that not one of them looked in my direction. You couldn't see through them.

The soldiers were small men 'about five feet [1.5m], in want of a good wash and shave. Nothing smart about them.' They were dressed in handmade uniforms 'like shirts, made of cloth, in various shades of green'. Martindale went on:

> When they came through the wall, I couldn't even see the horse from the knees down. The road had only been excavated in the centre of the cellar. The surface is 18 inches [45cm] below, and I couldn't see them from the feet up until they were walking on the centre of the cellar.
>
> They all had the same helmets on, with the plumes coming out of the back, down the neck. They all carried a short sword on the right-hand side. I used to think that Roman soldiers carried a long sword, but it was like an over-sized dagger on the right-hand side.
>
> The horse I can only describe as a great big cart horse – not like the chargers that they used nowadays on the television. And they came as quick as they went. When they were in the centre of the cellar, I could hear a murmuring, no speech, just a murmuring.

When the museum curator found the terrified boy collapsed at the top of the cellar steps, he immediately knew what had happened because he had seen the soldiers himself seven years before.

Above: Harry Martindale some years after he saw the ghostly soldiers.

Opposite: The Treasurer's House in York.

Below: The cellar beneath the Treasurer's House in York.

HAUNTED HOUSES

BUILDINGS OF ALL kinds and of all periods have experienced hauntings: churches, castles, abbeys, chapels, schools, factories and houses – both grand and humble, old and new. One example from the many intriguing reports is the haunting of St Anne's (see the photograph on the right), a large nineteenth-century house which still stands on the corner of Pittville Circus Road and All Saints Road in Cheltenham, Gloucestershire, UK. (It has now been converted into flats.) The Despard family moved into the house early in 1882 and, a few months later, 19-year-old Rosina Despard, who was studying medicine, began to see the ghost of a woman in black. She described her first encounter:

> I had gone up to my room, but was not yet in bed, when I heard someone at the door, and went to it, thinking it might be my mother. On opening the door, I saw no one; but on going a few steps along the passage, I saw the figure of a tall lady, dressed in black, standing at the head of the stairs. After a few moments, she descended the stairs, and I followed for a short distance, feeling curious what it could be. I had only a small piece of candle, and it suddenly burnt itself out; and being unable to see more, I went back to my room.

During the next two years, she saw the woman in black about six times and there were three appearances to other people. Rosina spoke to the ghost one day in the drawing-room, asking if she could help her:

> She moved, and I thought she was going to speak, but she only gave a slight gasp and moved towards the door. Just by the door I spoke to her again, but she seemed to disappear as before.

Whenever Rosina tried to touch her, she could not:

> It was not that there was nothing there to touch, but that she always seemed to be beyond me, and if followed into a corner, simply disappeared.

On several occasions Rosina fastened fine cords across the stairs which would be moved by a normal person, but she twice saw the woman in black pass through the cords, leaving them intact.

The behaviour of the dogs in the house suggested that they too were aware of the ghost. Rosina saw a Skye terrier run over to the stairs wagging its tail as if greeting someone. 'It jumped up, fawning as it would do if a person had been standing there, but suddenly slunk away with its tail between its legs, and retreated trembling, under a sofa. We were all strongly under the impression that it had seen the figure.'

Although the woman kept her face hidden by a handkerchief held in her right hand, they felt confident in identifying her as the ghost of Mrs Imogen Swinhoe, the widow of Henry Swinhoe, who had been the first occupant of the house from c.1860 until his death in 1876. Imogen was his second wife and theirs was a turbulent marriage, both of them being heavy drinkers. They quarrelled about the upbringing of Mr Swinhoe's children from his first marriage and Imogen left him a few months before his death. She died in 1878, aged 41 years. From the available details, it would appear that strong emotions were rampant in the house during the Swinhoes' occupation, which may be responsible for the presence of Imogen's ghost after her death.

POLTERGEISTS

Poltergeists have always been with us: there are recorded cases as far back as AD 530, and from all parts of the world. The German word *poltergeist* means literally 'noisy spirit', and that describes the behaviour of this phenomenon very well. Among its manifestations are banging noises, things being thrown around, furniture being piled up, and other destructive behaviour, such as attacking people and lighting fires; but it also expresses itself in other, quieter ways, such as hiding things or writing messages. It is seen as a mischievous spirit because that is what the behaviour suggests: a disembodied spirit that enjoys upsetting people. Just as there is no real evidence that ghosts are the spirits of the dead, so too is there nothing to prove that poltergeists are discarnate entities. It is clear that many poltergeist activities do not follow the rules laid down by science: things move without being touched, objects move slowly through the air, solid objects pass through other solid objects, spontaneous fires occur, water appears from nowhere, and so on. It is possible that these paranormal events are triggered by powers and energies we have not yet recognized, but which everyone has the potential to use.

ENFIELD POLTERGEIST

PROBABLY THE MOST famous British poltergeist in recent times was the Enfield poltergeist, which was at its most active in late 1977, reaching its climax in December. Its repertoire was impressive. It made knocking noises, moved furniture, threw things through the air, levitated children and threw them out of bed regularly, bent cutlery and left pools of water on the floor. It also communicated through knocks, by writing on paper and by speaking in a hoarse voice. The events were investigated by Guy Lyon Playfair and Maurice Grosse, who both witnessed many strange happenings. The photograph shows Maurice Grosse with some souvenirs from the case: the gas-fire was wrenched away from a wall, bending the half-inch brass gas-pipe.

STONE-THROWING POLTERGEISTS

SHOWERS OF STONES are often thrown in poltergeist cases and, despite strenuous efforts, their source can never be found. A particularly interesting occurrence began c.1979 and continued for several years in the Ward End area of Birmingham, UK. Five houses in Thornton Road were the focus of the attacks, being regularly bombarded with large stones. The residents had to board up their windows and erect mesh screens. The stones were similar to the ones found in the gardens, but they had no soil or fingerprints on them, as if they had been washed. The police spent months investigating the case: by the end of 1982 they had completed 3,500 man-hours of investigation. Despite constables spending cold nights huddled in sleeping-bags in the gardens and using night-sights, image-intensifiers and infra-red video, no clues were found. The policemen hiding in the gardens could hear the stones arriving but never discovered their source. The photographs show one of the affected houses in Thornton Road and some of the stones.

THIS photograph shows a stone from the Enfield poltergeist outbreak of 1977 (see p.79). Pieces of stone were thrown into the house in the presence of investigator Maurice Grosse, and he found that three pieces fitted together exactly, although the smallest piece arrived in the house several hours after the others. The pieces have been put back together for the photograph.

THE PHOTOGRAPH BELOW shows poltergeist investigator Guy Lyon Playfair at Carapicuiba in Brazil, in September 1974. He had received reports of mysterious stone-throwing and, on arrival, was told that the bombardment had been happening daily for more than three weeks, despite watches by police and residents. While he was standing talking, Playfair witnessed a hail of stones or pieces of brick falling out of a cloudless blue sky and in the photograph he shows a tile which had been broken by a stone only a few minutes before. He learned that a teenage girl lived in the house and she had received most of the attacks. This may provide a clue, since poltergeist activity often seems to focus on young people.

'POLTERGEIST GIRL'

Known as the 'poltergeist girl', Eleonore Zügun was a Romanian peasant born in 1913. In 1925, while she was on a visit to her grandmother, poltergeist phenomena broke out around Eleonore, and again when she arrived home. When parapsychologist Fritz Grunewald heard about the events, he had her removed to a monastery where he went to study the events. He recorded the movement of objects in her presence, and sometimes Eleonore was hit by them. She believed she was being plagued by a devil, Dracu. The phenomena, including the attacks by Dracu, continued when Eleonore was moved to Vienna for further study. As well as things being thrown at her, she was slapped, knocked over and thrown out of bed, her hair was pulled, her shoes filled with water, needles were stuck into her and she was scratched on her face, neck, arms and chest, these attacks leaving clearly visible marks (see the photograph above). Spittle would appear on her arms and face and, when analysed, it was found not to have come from her skin, nor from her mouth; her own saliva contained few micro-organisms, while that found on her skin was full of bacteria. Thankfully for Eleonore, the phenomena faded away in 1927 as she began to menstruate, suggesting that the turmoil of puberty somehow awoke the bizarre powers that afflicted her.

DODLESTON POLTERGEIST AND MESSAGES

THE STRANGE EVENTS at Dodleston, near Chester, UK, began in late 1984 and lasted for a couple of years. A small cottage which was home to a young couple, Ken and Debbie, became the focus of a poltergeist outbreak, with furniture being thrown around and small items, such as cat-food tins, being stacked up. As if this wasn't disturbing enough, events soon took a weird turn.

Domestic chaos caused by the Dodleston poltergeist.

The couple had a computer at the cottage (this was long before the time when it became commonplace to have a computer in the home and, in fact, it was on loan from the school where Ken taught) and Ken discovered a strange message on it, but they thought it must be a hoax and took no action. A few weeks later, when they borrowed the computer again, they found another, longer message, in old-fashioned language. When simplified, it read:

> I write on behalf of many. What strange words you speak, although, I must confess that I too have been badly educated. Sometimes it seems changes are somewhat obstructive, for many a time they disturb me sleeping in my bed. You are a worthy man who has a fanciful woman and you live in my house, I have no wish to alarm you, for it is only since the half-witted fool [?'antic' in the original] ripped apart my confines have I been tormented at nights. I have seen many changes (lastly the school house and your home). It is a fitting place, with lights which the devil makes, and costly things, which only my friend, Edmund Grey can afford, or the king himself. It was a great crime to have stolen my house. LW

'Lukas', as he later signed himself, became a regular correspondent and they learned that he was living in the sixteenth century in a cottage on the same site as theirs. They later learned that his real name was Tomas Harden. They also learned a great deal more about him as the long correspondence continued over the succeeding months. Clearly their renovation work on the cottage had stirred up powerful forces, causing both the poltergeist outbreak and apparently also opening a channel to the past. Not content with sending messages through the computer, Tomas also sometimes wrote them on the cottage floor.

As Ken and Debbie struggled to get to grips with the major mystery that had engulfed them, even stranger things began to happen. Debbie believed she actually met Tomas in some kind of trance state and the couple were now also getting messages from the year 2109. Finally the time came when Tomas had to sign off, because he had to leave his cottage, and the communications from 2109 also ceased. In all, during the period December 1984 to March 1987, about 300 messages were received, including those written in chalk. Ken's and Debbie's research went some way to verifying Tomas's story but, not surprisingly, because it is so incredible, many people found it difficult to believe and suspected that it was all an elaborate hoax. Ken and Debbie adamantly deny any involvement in a hoax: often there would be no one in the cottage when the messages came through on the computer (it was long before the days of e-mail). The events are described in Ken Webster's *The Vertical Plane* (1989), but so far no one has come up with a satisfactory explanation.

Part of a message from Tomas, written on the floor.

MULHOUSE POLTERGEIST

DURING 1977–81, a house in Mulhouse, France, was the focus of unexpected events: a young couple and their four-year-old son were experiencing poltergeist phenomena that included knockings at the windows, the sounds of crying babies and animals, a table 'dancing', bedclothes pulled off the bed and abrupt temperature changes. A physicist who was intrigued by the events installed a chart-recorder to continuously monitor the temperature, but the resulting lines on the print-out (see the photograph below) were not continuous, as they should have been, but broken and horizontal. Parapsychologist Dr Hans Bender was called in and he discovered that the

phenomena often centred on Carla. Like Eleonore Zügun (see p.81), she was physically attacked: punched in the stomach, pinched on the leg, scratched and cut on her face and arms, and even attempts made by 'cold hands' to strangle her. The investigators hypnotized Carla, hoping to film PK phenomena (see pp.105–6) that had been produced by post-hypnotic suggestion – but the equipment failed to work! Carla began to go into a trance state spontaneously and her husband kept a loaded camera close at hand so that he could photograph anything which might occur. He sealed the camera with tape, so that the film could not be interfered with, but, on one occasion when Carla entered a trance and he

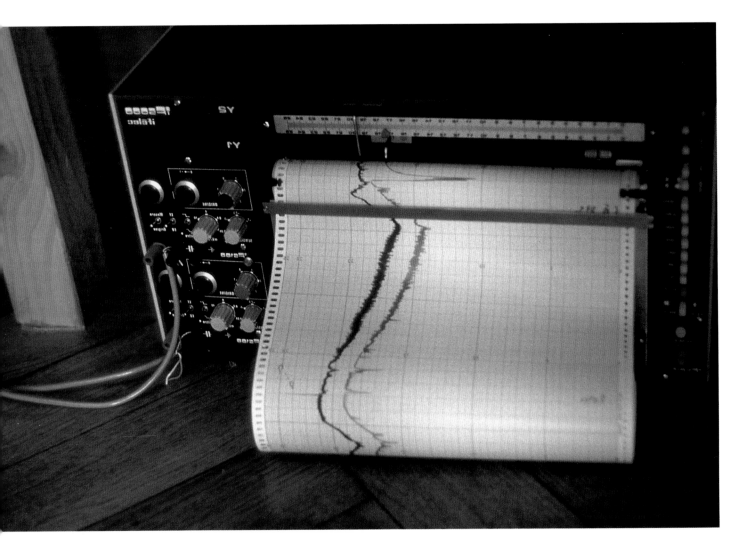

grabbed the camera, he discovered there was no film in it. Removing the tape, he found that the film had been replaced by a small, folded piece of paper with simple designs pencilled on it (shown in the inset right) – designs similar to those that had been found on the floor under the bed and as marks on Carla's thigh.

The investigators felt that the phenomena were due to some powerful force which focused on Carla. Suddenly she began to produce automatic drawings and the photograph below shows her holding a portrait of her young son. Her style changed with time and it seemed that the act of drawing had become an outlet to allow Carla to release bottled-up emotion. The couple eventually decided to leave the house and, as they packed their belongings, a neighbour informed them that the previous owner had experienced 'unexplained knockings and the mysterious opening and closing of doors', and that she had recently died. Perhaps the house was haunted and psychic energy given off by Carla had somehow triggered the poltergeist activity.

POLTERGEISTS IN BRAZIL

D URING THE EARLY 1970s, paranormal investigator Guy Lyon Playfair was living in Brazil, where he investigated numerous poltergeist outbreaks around the city of São Paulo (see also p.81). At Suzano in 1970, spontaneous fires were breaking out, and one witness told Playfair: 'If I live to be 100, I'll swear that the calendar hanging on the wall in front of my nose caught fire by itself. I even put my finger in the flame, to make sure it was real, and I burned my finger.' The photographs show a blanket which caught fire during this incident (below) and (right) slashed furniture, a result of the work of the Guarulhos poltergeist in 1973.

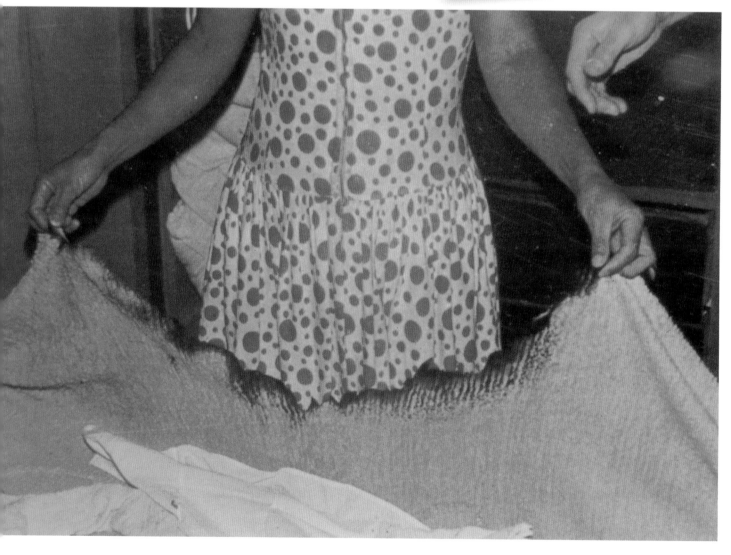

THIS PHOTOGRAPH WAS taken by Guy Lyon Playfair as the stool fell downstairs. He was sleeping in a poltergeist-haunted house in Ipiranga, again in São Paulo, in 1973, when he was woken by the stool falling into his room. He was able to ascertain that the only person upstairs was in her bedroom with the door closed. The stool had come from the other bedroom, where it was stored on top of a wardrobe. It had apparently come through a closed door; if the door had been open, the stairs would have been sunlit. Less than a minute later, a drawer of clothes was thrown out of the window of the same bedroom and, again, there was no one in the room. Poltergeist phenomena plagued the same family for six years, following them to four different homes.

SPIRIT PHOTOGRAPHY

In the last three decades of the nineteenth century and the early years of this century, so-called 'spirit photography' was all the rage. A living sitter would go to the studio of a medium with the gift of spirit photography and sit for a photograph; if he/she was lucky, there would also be another figure on the print, allegedly someone who was dead, possibly a family member. It was sometimes said that the image of the dead person did not resemble any known photograph. Of course trickery was often suspected and sometimes proved. The usual procedure was for the photographer to use a glass plate (which was used instead of flexible film in those days) onto which the spirit image had already been exposed. For this reason, sceptical sitters would take their own plates and try to ensure that the photographer did not switch them for ones he had prepared earlier.

T HE PHOTOGRAPH ABOVE shows parapsychol-
ogist Dr Gustave Geley (seated on the left) with S. De Porath, and the hand-written certification states that they had supplied their own plates, bought in London on that same day, opened by De Porath, signed, and not lost sight of during the whole process. In the same certificate he adds that the spirit image in the photograph was 'recognised by the lady's brother (non-spiritualist) and by three intimate friends. She "died" Aug. 1913. There is no similar portrait extant.' The photographer was William Hope, who was operating at Crewe, and he took this photograph in November 1919. It is, of course, possible that Hope and other spirit photographers had other ways of cheating, and opinion is divided as to whether he was genuine or not.

THE PHOTOGRAPH ABOVE was also taken at Crewe, *c.*1922, by a member of the same circle of mediums to which William Hope belonged. It shows a Liverpool couple with the spirit image of their dead son; to the right is a photograph of the boy as he was *c.*1916. The likeness is undeniable, but this cannot prove the authenticity of the spirit photograph.

MEDIUMS, ECTOPLASM AND SPIRITS

ECTOPLASM

ECTOPLASM (OR TELEPLASM) HAS been defined as 'a mysterious protoplasmic substance' which streams from any opening in the medium's body, often shaping itself into spirit forms.

THE PHOTOGRAPH BELOW shows the famous American medium 'Margery' (Mrs Crandon), with her hands being held and ectoplasm apparently issuing from her ear.

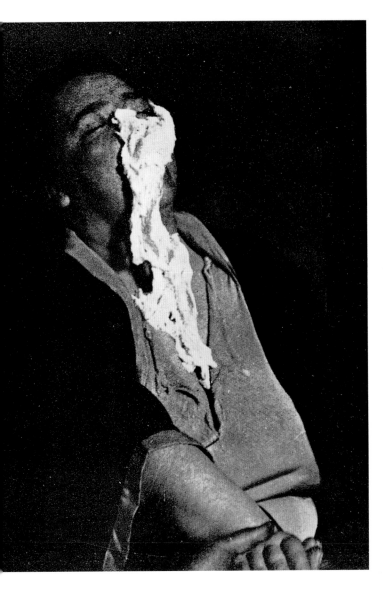

To the left is Mary M., a Canadian medium, with ectoplasm draped over her face. 'Draped' is a carefully chosen word, since sceptics believed that the ectoplasm was cheesecloth, or something similar, which the medium had swallowed and then regurgitated. If the test with Margery Crandon (shown opposite) is faked, then clearly the people holding her hands are in on the hoax.

Sometimes the ectoplasm would form itself into faces or even whole figures. The close-up of an ectoplasmic face (right) shows the French medium known as Eva C., around whose abilities controversy raged. Some eminent parapsychologists, such as Albert von Schrenk-Notzing, believed her to be genuine, but others were equally convinced that she faked the phenomena. Although this face and many other allegedly ectoplasmic figures look like blatant fakes, some investigators did not consider that this meant they *were* fakes. They said that the two-dimensional figures look like still-lifes in photographs but, to those present, they looked alive and were moving and changing.

SCOTTISH MEDIUM Helen Duncan's ectoplasmic figure (below) is connected to her face by a long cord of ectoplasm; note that her hands are being controlled, so again, if this is a hoax, the controllers must also have been part of it. Despite the support of many followers who believed her to be genuine, Helen Duncan was caught cheating. Her 'ectoplasm' was said to be made of cheesecloth, wood pulp and white of egg. X-rays proved that she swallowed it before a seance and then regurgitated it as necessary. In 1932, she was caught hoaxing when, during a seance, a child she had allegedly materialized was grabbed by a sitter and found to be the medium herself. In 1944 Helen Duncan was taken to court and charged with claiming falsely to be in contact with the spirits of the dead. She was found guilty.

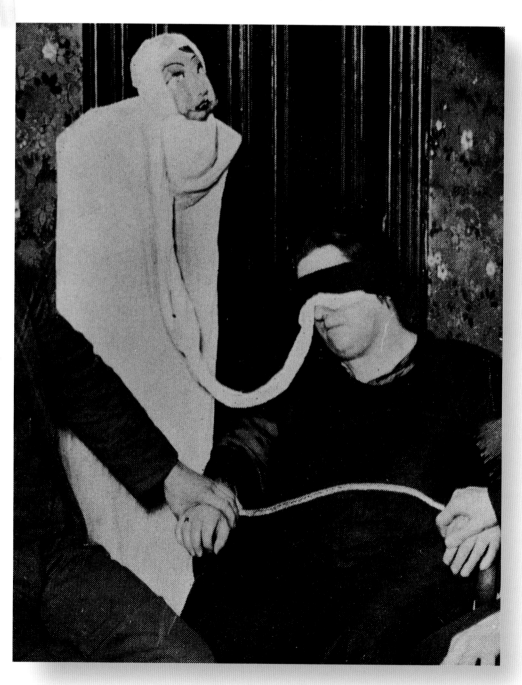

MATERIALIZATIONS

SPIRITUALISM ACTUALLY BEGAN in the mid-1850s in the USA and has remained popular ever since, although its heyday was in the late nineteenth and early twentieth centuries. The materialization of spirits began *c*.1860 and one of the most famous spirits was Katie King (shown in the photograph), who appeared at Florence Cook's seances in 1874. The events of Cook's mediumship became famous because they were investigated and endorsed by scientist Sir William Crookes, who claimed that he saw both the medium and the spirit together. He made notes at the time, and later wrote:

> I went cautiously into the room [after Katie had given him permission to enter the cabinet], it being dark, and felt about for Miss Cook. I found her crouching on the floor. Kneeling down, I let air enter the phosphorus lamp, and by its light I saw the young lady dressed in black velvet as she had been in the early part of the evening, and to all appearances perfectly senseless; she did not move when I took her hand and held the light quite close to her face, but continued quietly breathing. Raising the lamp I looked around and saw Katie standing close behind Miss Cook. She was robed in flowing white drapery as we had seen her previously during the seance. Holding one of Miss Cook's hands in mine, and still kneeling, I passed the lamp up and down so as to illuminate Katie's whole figure, and satisfy myself thoroughly that I was really looking at the veritable Katie whom I had clasped in my arms a few minutes before and not at the phantasm of a disordered brain. She did not speak but moved her head and smiled in recognition. Three separate times did I carefully examine Miss Cook . . . to be sure that the hand I held was that of a living woman, and three separate times did I turn the lamp to Katie and examine her with steadfast scrutiny until I had no doubt whatever of her objective reality.

He also noted that a blister on Miss Cook's neck was not present on Katie's neck and that only Miss Cook's ears were pierced. Sir William also claimed to have seen Katie King and another spirit together in his laboratory, walking arm in arm. The other spirit was 'Florence', the control of medium Rosina Showers, whom Crookes later accepted was a fraud, although he does not appear to have concluded that therefore Florence Cook was also a fraud. When Katie King stopped appearing, she was followed by other materializations, one of which was seized by Sir George Sitwell during a seance in 1880, who found himself holding Florence Cook in her underwear. She was also caught cheating on other occasions. Nevertheless some people still believe that Katie King was a genuine materialization.

Katie King.

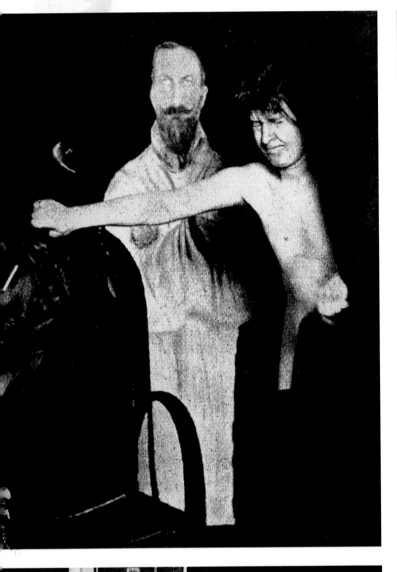

Above left: Eva C., photographed with a two-dimensional materialization in 1913 (see p.91).

Above right: William Eglinton with a fully materialized spirit c.1878 (he was another medium who, some believed, achieved his results by trickery).

Left: Famous Polish medium Franek Kluski at a Warsaw seance in 1919, with a strange monster-like figure materialized at his right shoulder.

THIS PHOTOGRAPH SEEMS too unbelievable, but is claimed to show the materialization of the dead poet Giuseppe Parini, sitting between the South American medium Carlo Mirabelli, who is in a trance (seated on the left), and Dr Carlos de Castro of the Cesar Lombroso Academy of Psychic Studies in Brazil (seated on the right).

Their report, following their investigation of Mirabelli's powers, claimed that he was able to produce materialized spirits, levitate in broad daylight and move objects using psychokinesis, as well as producing automatic writing and speaking in 26 languages. The figures he materialized were examined by doctors and found to be perfectly formed. On one occasion, it was claimed, he materialized Bishop Dr José de Carmago Barros who had died in a shipwreck. One person present later wrote:

A sweet smell as of roses filled the room. The medium went into trance. A fine mist was seen in the circle. The mist, glowing as if of gold, parted and the bishop materialised, with all the robes and insignia of office. He called his own name. Dr de Souza stepped to him. He palpated the body, touched his teeth, tested the saliva, listened to the heart-beat, investigated the working of the intestines [how?!], nails and eyes, without finding anything amiss . . . Then he slowly dematerialised.

Needless to say, other researchers felt that the Academy's report was less than objective and that Mirabelli couldn't have done all the things claimed or, at least, not without accomplices. He died in 1951, so the truth will probably never be known.

STRANGE POWERS

INTRODUCTION

SCIENCE HAS ALWAYS denied the possibility of paranormal powers because they do not follow the objective rules that scientists have laid down. It is often assumed that scientists would be eager to investigate new possibilities, but this seems rarely to be the case. Scientists, like everyone else, don't want to be seen to be making fools of themselves and so, when faced with evidence of some strange new power, they feel safer saying: 'This is not possible!' Their attitude is that, if something cannot be replicated to order, it is therefore unscientific, and so they ignore it, rather than saying, as they should in the true spirit of science: 'This sounds interesting – let's look into it!'

The scientists' attitude towards paranormal powers is especially regrettable because such powers have the potential to change our lives in a major and positive way, if only they were understood and utilized. Scientists might argue that they have investigated the paranormal and the results were no better than could be expected by chance, but such subtle forces may be influenced in ways that science would not recognize, for example by a negative attitude. If a scientist performs an experiment expecting it not to work – behold! – the result is negative or inconclusive. Then someone with a positive attitude performs the same experiment and the results are better than would be expected if only chance were at work – so the scientists claim that the experiment was not correctly regulated and is therefore invalid. By their refusal to redefine their procedures and investigate the paranormal impartially, scientists are isolating themselves from a wide range of human experience and holding back the development of the potentialities of paranormal powers.

Coincidentally, as this piece was being written, a newspaper item caught our attention. Headed 'Science proves power of mind over matter', it describes experiments conducted at Princeton University in the USA, which have demonstrated the reality of psychokinesis (PK). Compared with some of the dramatic ways in which PK energies can be demonstrated, the experiments performed at Princeton over 12 years seem rather boring, and the danger with boring laboratory experiments in this field is that the participants will lose interest and their powers will not manifest themselves. In these experiments, an electronic random number generator produced sequences of ones and zeros. The subjects were asked to try and change the numbers using the power of thought. In normal circumstances, an equal number of ones and zeros would be produced over a long period, but these experiments seem to show that PK can affect the expected outcome. The experimenters performed thousands of trials over the years, using over 100 subjects.

The success of the Princeton experiments follows another apparently successful series of experiments carried out at Edinburgh University, Scotland, in which positive results were obtained from experiments to test whether telepathy (one person sending an image to another using only the mind) works. It seems that the tide is slowly turning in favour of the reality of paranormal powers. However, the doubters will never concede an inch, even in the face of scientifically respectable and impressive evidence.

After the Princeton results were released, one doubter commented: 'The effect sizes are so staggeringly small that some people would argue that any sensible person would prefer a non-PK explanation. There's also a worry that with the huge number of trials needed, conventional statistical theory starts to break down.' In fact, any sensible person would say: 'Yes, there seems to be an effect, even though it is only small: we must do more experiments.' And as for the suggestion that the large number of experiments means that the statistics are no longer reliable, we seem to recall that, in the past, experimenters have been criticized for not carrying out enough experiments.

It is good news that, at last, established scientists are exploring paranormal effects and trying to understand how they operate. Soon, perhaps, these phenomena will be used for the benefit of humanity. Meanwhile, let us have a look at what these powers are supposed to be able to do.

Telepathy and clairvoyance go together, as they both involve the power of the mind to obtain and convey information. Using telepathy, or mind-reading, some people can receive images being 'sent' by another person at a distance – and it doesn't seem to matter how far that distance is. Clairvoyance (literally 'clear seeing') is the ability to obtain information about hidden events and again the distance is no object. Precognition is similar to clairvoyance but, in this case, the events that are perceived are still in the future. Telepathy, clairvoyance and precognition all come under the heading of extrasensory perception (ESP). Some people claim to be psychic, to be sensitive to non-physical influences, to possess the power to communicate with the dead. The last group are known as mediums, whose powers have already been illustrated (see pp.90–5). However, there are other ways in which psychic powers manifest themselves. Some people produce psychic art or psychic music, and others produce automatic writing. Psychic healing is one of the ways in which gifted people use their powers for the good of others.

Psychokinesis is the power to affect objects using the power of the mind (see pp.105–6). Such effects can also be seen in poltergeist outbreaks, for example when furniture is moved, and illustrations showing this effect have been shown (see pp.79–87). PK is also believed to be responsible for such varied abilities as metal-bending, levitation, and thoughtography (whereby a person can produce a photographic image by mind-power alone). Levitation can be of small or large inanimate objects, or it can be of a person's body. Linked to this is the out-of-body experience (OBE), or astral projection, in which a person seems to leave his/her body. If all these abilities one day become scientifically respectable, humanity will enter a new age and all the scientific developments we have marvelled at in the twentieth century (especially computers) may then appear to be very primitive.

Another way in which people's strange powers manifest themselves is through religious phenomena – such as visions of the Virgin Mary, miracle cures, bleeding stigmata (Christ's wounds), and religious pictures and statues that mysteriously weep and bleed – though the full picture has not yet been deciphered, nor is there any agreement about whether any external influence is at work.

TELEPATHY AND CLAIRVOYANCE

THE TWO PHOTOGRAPHS show experiments that do not involve any distance, yet are no less impressive. The one on the left, taken in 1989, shows 15-year-old Monica Nieta Tejada, a Spanish girl who can clairvoyantly see words hidden in a sealed box. She concentrates on the box, holding it in her hands, and then writes down the word she has seen. In this instance she wrote 'truth', and her guess was successful; both the target and her guess are shown here. The other photograph shows Velibor, a young boy psychic from the former Yugoslavia, taking part in an ESP experiment and being watched by the parapsychologist who discovered him. Velibor can read letters and numbers inside sealed envelopes.

Mental abilities such as telepathy and clairvoyance are difficult to illustrate photographically because there is nothing to see except a person concentrating! In both abilities, distance is no object, and information can be acquired from the other side of the world with no time delay. I (Janet Bord) proved that to my own satisfaction not long ago, when watching a televised telepathy experiment. A man in the USA was looking at a picture and transmitting it to Uri Geller in a London television studio. I was in Wales and I 'saw' enough details of the picture to be convinced that I had received a telepathic image. The implications are pretty mind-boggling, because our present scientific knowledge does not encompass such 'impossible' happenings.

PSYCHIC CREATIVITY

AUTOMATIC WRITING

THERE IS NO conscious control when automatic writing is happening: something or someone else has taken over. Some people believe that discarnate spirits control the pen; others believe that the writer's unconscious is producing the message. An Italian lady, Anita (seen above), produces messages with information that she cannot possibly know. Although right-handed, she holds the pen on the open palm of her left hand to write automatically. One of the messages told her what had happened to a man who had disappeared. It said that he had become the victim of a crime and drew a location some distance from his home. When the information was followed up, human remains were found. The photograph (above right) showing two different types of writing has an automatic message at the top, signed by Anita's spirit guide. Below is the same message, written in her normal handwriting.

AUTOMATIC ART

SOME MEDIUMS HAVE expressed themselves through painting and often the artworks produced are unusual and of a high quality. Each medium interprets his/her work differently. Milly Canavero interpreted her drawings as symbols of spiritual evolution sent by a trans-galactic entity, while Clara Schuff said that her automatic artworks represented hieroglyphs, symbols and images from highly developed civilizations long disappeared from the Earth. She would speak in the languages of these people and then produce her automatic drawings.

The mediumistic artist Narciso Bressanello (shown below), from Venice, Italy, used to be a ship-repairer. Later in his life he felt the urge to paint and believed that someone else was painting through him. He sometimes reads or listens to music, and draws on large sheets of paper according to the rhythm of the text or music. He has produced thousands of drawings and paintings in which he has developed his own mythology and cosmology. For example, some of his paintings include little lines, like spines, on the houses and ships, which Bressanello says represent prayers, as a kind of protection.

Below: Mediumistic artist Narciso Bressanello.

Opposite: The regal head is a painting by psychic artist Heinrich Nüsslein and it shows the king of an unknown trans-galactic civilization.

THE MODIGLIANI-STYLE painting shown below was done by Brazilian trance-artist Luiz Gasparetto, who can very quickly produce new paintings in the style of classical artists, such as Leonardo da Vinci or Rembrandt, and more recent artists like Modigliani and Picasso. He sometimes does more than one at a time: one artist coming through one hand, another through the other hand, and a third through his feet! He can also do paintings upside down, and often looks away while painting. He believes that the paintings are channelled through him so that he can prove that there is life after death. After getting a telepathic invitation to paint, he says that a force overpowers his arms, which then move automatically.

AUTOMATIC MUSIC

Rosemary Brown became famous because of her alleged ability to produce new music dictated by dead composers. The photograph shows her in October 1980, writing down a mazurka composed by Chopin. The experts disagree about the music she produces. Some say it is banal; others believe it is genuine. One theory is that the music comes from Rosemary Brown's unconscious mind, a theory supported by the fact that the flow can be interrupted at any time when domestic duties call. Also, it seems strange that Hungarian, Polish, Austrian and German composers would choose an unknown widow from London, UK, as a channel for their new compositions. On the other hand, if the other experts are correct and the music really does originate from dead composers, a major reappraisal of the nature of death is required.

MIND OVER MATTER

The latest scientific experiments seem to show that we really can control inanimate objects using only the power of the mind, or psychokinesis (PK). The positive results announced in 1997 are only the latest to come from a long line of laboratory experiments; even back in the 1920s, PK experiments were taking place.

THE BLACK-AND-WHITE photograph on the left shows one of Dr Albert von Schrenck-Notzing's experiments in the 1920s with the Polish medium Stanislawa Tomczyk. In a state of half-trance, she could move small objects such as matchboxes, pencils, spoons and, as shown, balls; she could also produce lights, mark photographic plates and precipitate chemicals held in solution – all by the power of her mind.

This photograph shows a more recent event as Leonhard Hochenegg lights a neon tube simply by holding it in his bare hands.

URING THE LAST 25 years the best-known demonstration of PK power has been metal-bending and its most famous exponent is Uri Geller (right). He is an Israeli psychic, now living in the UK, who, in addition to spoon-bending, has used his abilities to start broken clocks and watches and affect all kinds of equipment. He can also 'see' things using extrasensory perception (ESP) and telepathy, and has taken part in numerous scientific experiments. He has used his powers to dowse for minerals for large international companies. Despite his many successes, sceptics claim that he uses fraudulent methods rather than psychic powers.

ONICA NIETO TEJADA (left), who was shown earlier performing an experiment in ESP or clairvoyance (see p.100), could also bend metal using her PK powers. In 1989 experiments, a metal strip was placed in a sealed glass container, which she held. After a while, the strip was found to have bent.

HUMAN MAGNETISM

WHILE IN MOSCOW working on a documentary on Russian parapsychology in March 1994, Kevin P. Braithwaite visited the apartment of leading para-psychologist Edward Naumov. During their discussions the subject of human magnetism came up and Naumov offered to give Kevin a demonstration, with him as the subject. He later described what happened:

Above: Edward Naumov demonstrating human magnetism to Kevin Braithwaite.

> After taking my shirt off, I made sure that my chest and skin was not in any way 'sticky'. He proceeded to place various cutlery on my chest, while asking me to concentrate. The more I seemed to concentrate the better the objects 'stuck'. Two other people were observers that evening and noted that the forks slightly resisted any attempt to remove them as if they were magnetic. With the later objects (two small irons) I found that my earlier inhibitions and doubts proved detrimental and stopped any 'attraction'. The more mentally composed I became the better they stuck, much to Edward's satisfaction. However since then I have tried to repeat the demonstration in private and have had no success whatsoever, thereby signifying that Naumov was indeed some form of 'energiser'.

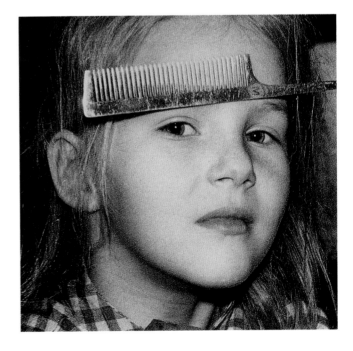

ANOTHER EXAMPLE of human magnetism comes from the same part of the world and shows an eight-year-old girl (probably in the 1980s) who could hold combs, tea-spoons and other small objects on her forehead.

THOUGHTOGRAPHY

'Thoughtography' is the name given to the power, demonstrated by some mediums, to produce photographs simply by the power of thought. In that respect it must have some link with psychokinesis.

IN 1910 THOUGHTOGRAPHY experiments were conducted in Japan by Professor Fukurai, but the best-known exponent of thoughtography was Ted Serios, a colourful character from Chicago, USA, who would stare into the lens of a Polaroid camera while thinking about the target subject. The resulting photograph would often show a blurred scene or building. He was naturally accused of cheating, especially because he preferred to use what he called his 'gismo' while making pictures. This was a small plastic tube that he would hold in front of the camera lens. It was examined by Dr Jules Eisenbud, who tested Serios over a couple of years in the 1960s, but nothing suspicious could be found.

One of the psychic photographs obtained by Glendinning and Duguid in 1896.

Even before the Japanese experiments, mediums were claiming to be able to produce psychic photographs. Scottish investigator Andrew Glendinning called the photographs he obtained in 1896 through the medium David Duguid 'dorcha-graphs', a name which luckily did not survive into the twentieth century! Glendinning would open a new box of glass plates (which were used for photography before the introduction of film) and place one of them, still in its paper wrapping, into the medium's hands, then put his own hands around those of the medium. Duguid likened the sensation to holding the handle of a magnetic battery while a slight current passed through it. Then the plate was developed and a figure would sometimes be found on it. The method described sounds foolproof, but we cannot be sure that Duguid did not somehow swap plates, substituting one he had prepared earlier before the plate was developed. The reason we should not accept these experiments at face value is because another aspect of Duguid's mediumship involved producing small paintings in the darkness of the seance room. He began doing automatic painting in 1866 and witnesses testified to the fact that the paintings were wet when produced. There were also other safeguards employed. However, in 1905 he was caught cheating, having brought prepared paintings to a seance. This happened at the end of his career, after nearly 2,000 seances – and the 'dorchagraph' experiments were not many years earlier. It is possible that Duguid felt his powers waning and felt it necessary to help them along by cheating. The truth will never be known.

Writer and editor, W. T. Stead was a firm supporter of spiritualism; he died in the *Titanic* disaster in 1912. His daughter, Estelle, was also involved in spiritualism and one day in October 1924, just before leaving home for the seance she regularly attended, she received news of the death of her uncle. During the journey to the seance, she mentally requested her dead father for some sign that he and his brother were now reunited. She asked that this be done on the photographic plates which were to be exposed that evening. The resulting photograph (right) was considered to be the desired proof, for it shows the letters W and J joined by a hyphen. J was the initial of her uncle's name and W was that of her father's. The medium, Mrs Deane, was responsible for the photograph, which was obtained without exposing the plate to light. Unfortunately it is not known whether Mrs Deane was aware of Estelle's request to her dead father. The two worked together over a number of years and Estelle testified to Mrs Deane's integrity:

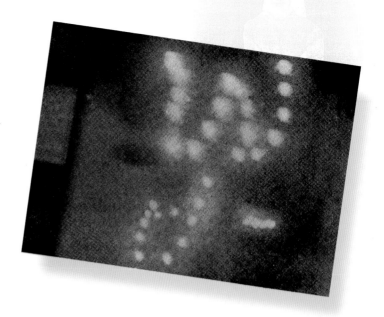

> I have known Mrs Deane and worked with her for the last four years [this was possibly written in 1924] and have the highest regard for her honesty and integrity of purpose. I know her cameras well, both inside and out, having examined them so often – also the dark slides used for these sittings. Both cameras and slides are continually left in my studio for days together, and I and others have plenty of opportunities to examine them at our leisure. The plates are always developed in my darkroom, and I can assure those doughty champions who explain so glibly how these are 'faked' that there are no developing dishes with transparent xylonite bases let into the dark-room table, nor any concealed electric lights in my dark room. We use porcelain dishes, which are washed out after every sitting.

Although suspicions must always remain, nothing can be proved at this late date.

IN THE 1950s, psychic photographs were being obtained in the USA by Raymond Welsh and his wife Margaret E. W. Fleming. The photographs were made without using film or a camera, but simply by holding a piece of photographic paper and concentrating on the picture desired. This was done in a darkroom, and the paper was then exposed to a 60-watt white bulb for a quick count of two, and then immersed in developer. When the picture started to form, the paper was removed, rinsed in clear water and then put into hypo for ten minutes. Pictures of people were often obtained, but nothing was known about them. The gruesome photograph below appears to show a dead body.

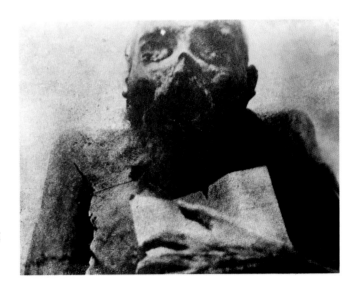

PSYCHIC HEALING

Psychic healers practise their art using many different methods, but all depend upon some interchange between healer and patient. Opinions differ as to the source of the power harnessed by the healer: it could be God, or some other external force, or it could come from the healer him/herself. Whatever its source, the successful healer appears to be able to utilize some energy and channel it into the patient so that it reinforces the patient's own natural power of healing. The energy can also be used against bacteria, as has been demonstrated in successful experiments in which a psychic has placed his/her hands on top of a bottle containing a solution of *E. coli* bacteria and tried to inhibit their growth.

NICOLA CUTOLO IS an Italian psychic who performs healing using the laying-on of hands (below right). He also uses a pendulum on photographs of patients to diagnose their illnesses (below left). He has been tested by Professor Fritz Albert Popp at the Institute for Biophysical Cell Research in Germany. Popp has developed a machine to make biophotons (light transmitted through living cells) visible and, at that time, Cutolo was the only subject out of several hundreds tested who could increase the biophoton discharge in the palm of his hand. Some people believe that biophotons play a vital role in healing.

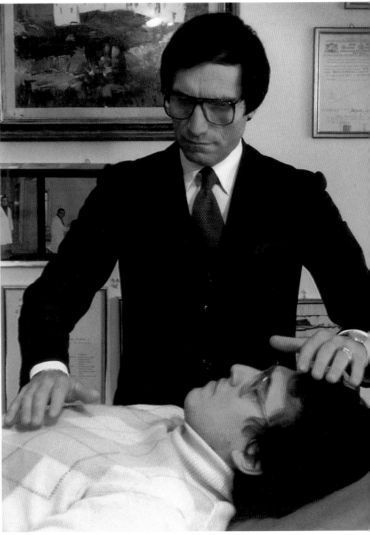

PSYCHIC SURGERY IS a very different method of alternative healing that has been known about since the 1950s. Chiefly practised in the Philippines, Brazil and other South American countries, the surgeons operate on their patients in non-sterile conditions using rusty knives and without anaesthetics. They are often in a trance-like state. They apparently push their hands into the patient's body and bring out a bloody mass of tissue. The wound heals instantly and the patient can get up and walk away. No post-operative infection is reported. Although this sounds impossible, many investigators who have observed this surgery have reported being unable to find evidence of hoaxing by the most famous healers (although inevitably cheats have also been exposed). The photograph shows Ivan Trilha, a psychic surgeon from Paraguay, at work in 1979.

SINCE 1988, SCIENTISTS at the Paramann Programme Laboratories in Jordan have been testing dervishes from the Sufi School of Tariqa Casnazaniyyah ('the way that is known to no one') because of their ability to injure themselves and heal the wounds within seconds (see the photograph below). Their brainwaves were monitored as they stabbed themselves with daggers, pierced themselves with skewers, swallowed glass and razor blades, burned themselves for 5–15 seconds, were bitten by poisonous snakes and scorpions, and more. A few drops of blood would appear on the wound, but in all cases the wounds would heal within seconds and there were no infections, even though the instruments they used were not sterilized. However, if a dervish should be *accidentally* injured, he suffered the same pain, bleeding, infection, and so on, as any other person. Writing in 1996, the Director of the Laboratory said that people performing DCBD (deliberately caused bodily damage) feats need not be in any special state of mind.

> The dervishes that we experimented upon *do not* enter any altered state of consciousness before, during, or after their performances. This was confirmed by the normality of their EEG [electroencephalograph] recordings. DCBD phenomena seem to suggest that mind–body interaction can take place on a much subtler level than sharp alternation in consciousness.

He added that some dervishes seemed able to transfer their DCBD abilities to another person, controlling that person while he or she was injured, so that no pain or bleeding would be felt. If such things can be proved to happen under scientific test conditions, then perhaps psychic surgery (see p.111) is not impossible after all.

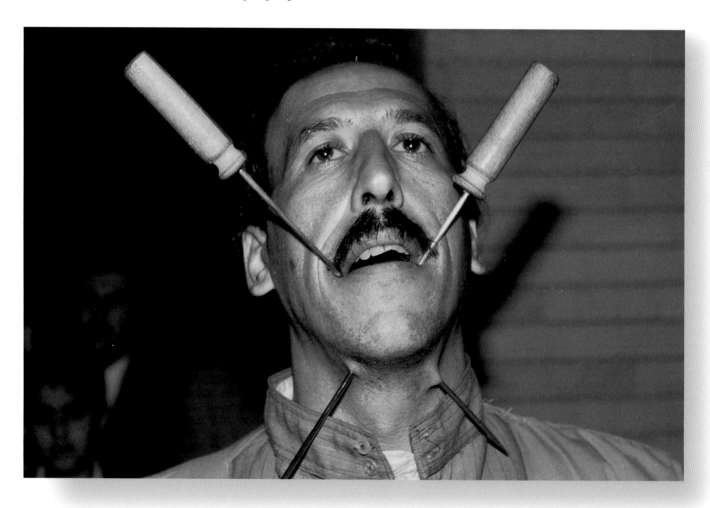

GROWING COPPER FOIL

IN THE 1980s Dr Berthold E. Schwarz, a psychic researcher in Florida, USA, reported that a woman called Katie had frequently found copper foil developing on her skin (see the photograph below). She also had various psychic abilities that Dr Schwarz was studying, such as metal-bending, levitation of objects, writing medieval French while in a trance, precognition, and the appearance of marks like crosses, Viking ships, and burns on her skin.

Katie was often in a trance state, during sessions with the doctor at her home and in his office, when the copper started to appear. He noted the copper on her face, neck, hands, chest, back and abdomen. Sometimes it also appeared on her lip and tongue, but the doctor stressed that he examined her mouth before the experiments, and she drank some water, so it was not possible for her to be regurgitating the copper.

Dr Schwarz pulled some of the foil off Katie's skin, just like peeling sunburned skin away, and this caused her some discomfort. The foil was chemically analysed and found to be approximately 98 per cent copper and 2 per cent zinc. On a few occasions the foil also developed independently of Katie. When she was trying to help sick people using psychic healing, a few flecks of copper were seen to appear on their skin. On one occasion at his office, Dr Schwarz made a cup of coffee for Katie and she stood it on a table to cool down. When she picked it up again, a fleck of copper was seen floating on top of the coffee. Dr Schwarz kept the cup and three days later the copper was still present.

Among the experiments that Dr Schwarz attempted with Katie was one using a tamper-proof sealed bottle containing two aortic rings (made from animal blood vessels). She was to take the bottle home and try, paranormally, to make the rings link up. On this occasion she also took home a second sealed bottle. When she got home and unpacked the bottles, she found that there was foil, which seemed to be growing, in the second bottle. Dr Schwarz checked that the bottle fastening had not been tampered with. He wondered if perhaps the foil had somehow been materialized, or 'apported' (paranormally transferred), into the bottle by Katie.

This strange appearance of copper foil on the skin of someone who has psychic powers is very unusual, but it may be in some way similar to the ectoplasm which some spiritualist mediums at the turn of the century could produce (see p.90). As with Katie when she produced the copper, the medium would have been in a trance when she produced ectoplasm but, while Katie's copper foil remained afterwards, the ectoplasm soon disappeared. Although critics who have never seen these phenomena say that they were faked, people who were present were convinced that something very strange was happening.

113

EASTERN POWERS

In the East, the same powers of 'mind over matter' are demonstrated as in the West, but there such powers are not so exceptional.

THE YOGI WITH his head buried in the sand (above) has reduced his breathing to zero and his pulse rate has dropped to two beats per minute. In effect, he is in a state of suspension. This photograph was taken in November 1974 at Agra in India.

ALSO IN INDIA, the swami at Mahabalipuram is performing 'miracles' by materializing objects from his mouth. The photograph shows him materializing a stone lingam (a Hindu symbol), but he also produced for the photographer some very long threads and a plant (the latter *not* from his mouth!). There is a clear difference between the swami's skills, which could be ascribed to sleight of hand, and the yogi's ability to put himself into suspension. The swami's alleged powers are akin to those of Western mediums (see pp.90–95).

THIS PHOTOGRAPH, TAKEN in 1991, shows an event from a magical trance-dance performed on the island of Java, Indonesia. The men perform a dance with a hobby horse (which itself is an intriguing link with hobby-horse dances traditionally performed in England, for example at Padstow in Cornwall on May Day), accompanied by a Javanese gamelan orchestra. In a trance state, the dancers can perform unusual feats and injure themselves without feeling pain. The photographer saw one man stripping a coconut with his bare teeth, eating broken glass from a light bulb and having a large needle pushed through his cheek, which is shown in the photograph.

LEVITATION

As human beings don't have wings, it would seem to be impossible for them to fly, yet some have claimed this ability.

THE MOST FAMOUS recent example of bodily levitation must be the medium D. D. Home, who, in 1868, is said to have floated out of a third-floor window of a London house and in again through a window of the adjoining room. There must, however, be some doubt as to whether this really happened.

Another medium who allegedly possessed the power to levitate was the Italian Amedee Zuccarini, and flash photographs were taken of him in the air. The photograph shown here (right) is interesting, but the blurring shows he was in motion rather than hovering and perhaps he was able to leap or spring up from a sitting position.

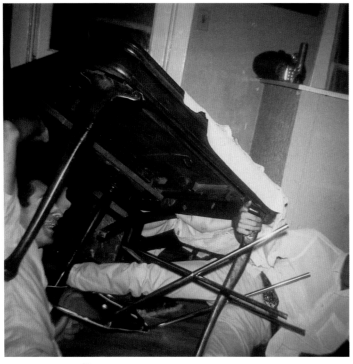

RATHER MORE BELIEVABLE are the many reports of tables and other inanimate objects moving without human influence. Poltergeist reports (see p.79) often describe objects moving without being touched by anyone. A group known as SORRAT (Society for Research on Rapport and Telekinesis), which has been experimenting in Missouri, USA, for over 35 years, has experienced countless table levitations, but the event which took place on 7 June 1966 was particularly dramatic. That evening, a small metal table had been 'walking' around, indoors and out. It went into the dining room and under the 80lb (36.2kg), six-legged wooden table. Ray Christ and Joe Mangini leaned down to look for it. Suddenly the wooden table levitated upwards (see left) to a height of 4ft (1.2m), hovered for a moment, then crashed to the floor, breaking off two legs.

FLYING SAINTS

Saints in a state of ecstatic trance have been lifted into the air and remained suspended for some while, or so it has been reported. St Teresa (1515-82) described the sensation of being in the state of ecstasy or rapture:

> It comes, in general, as a shock, quick and sharp, before you can collect your thoughts, or help yourself in any way, and you see and feel it as a cloud, or a strong eagle rising upwards and carrying you away on its wings.

She would resist the rapture, especially when it came over her in public, but felt worn out afterwards. She also said:

> At other times it was impossible to resist at all; my soul was carried away, and almost always my head with it – I had no power over it – and now and then the whole body as well, so that it was lifted up from the ground.

On one occasion, when she felt the rapture coming over her during a church service, she threw herself on the ground and the nuns came to hold her down.

> After the rapture was over, I have to say that my body seemed frequently to be buoyant, as if all weight had departed from it, so much so that now and then I scarcely knew that my feet touched the ground.

Even more remarkable was the case of St Joseph of Copertino (1603-63) who was said to be literally able to fly (see right), as was observed more than a hundred times. Eye-witnesses described how he would fly up 7 or 8ft (2 or 2.5m) in order to kiss the statue of the Infant Jesus over the altar; he also carried this wax image in his arms and floated around with it. Once he caught up another friar and carried him around the room. Very soon after his death, the witnesses confirmed under oath that they had seen St Joseph levitate.

OUT-OF-BODY EXPERIENCES

Would your friends believe you if you told them you could leave your body lying asleep and travel wherever you wanted to go instantaneously? Probably not, but many people claim that this has happened to them.

THIS EXPERIENCE USED to be called 'astral projection', but now it is usually known as an out-of-the-body experience, or OBE. A few people are able to have such an experience whenever they wish, but most experiencers say that it happens unexpectedly. For example, one woman said:

> One afternoon I felt unusually tired so I went to lie on my bed taking with me my little cat, who settled beside me washing himself. Suddenly I became aware of rings of cloudiness around his head and I realised I was floating high above him looking down. My own body was also there on the bed. I felt lonely and afraid because I imagined I would never get back. When I seemed to panic I was in my body again.

Another woman, living in Surrey, England, had an OBE when she was worried about her son in Canada, from whom she had not heard for a while. She explained what happened:

> One night I couldn't have been long asleep when suddenly I found I was floating about four feet [1.2m] above my bed, and on looking down I could see myself sleeping beside my husband . . . then suddenly I seemed to shoot through the ceiling and found myself moving rapidly through the air, lying on my back. After a while I could see I was moving over water, then I crossed huge plains, and finally forests of trees . . . somehow I sensed my son was not there, and the next thing I knew I landed on my bed again with such a bump that I not only woke myself, but my husband as well. He always maintained that the bed jumped at least a foot [12cm] off the floor.

This white shape is said to be someone's swaying astral body, photographed during experiments into astral projection.

Next morning she drew a picture of the place she had seen, and her son, when he saw it, said it was exactly right.

The people whose descriptions we read have always come back to their bodies – but are there people who have not come back? In other words, is this experience the same as dying? Some people who have left their bodies claim to have seen dead friends and relations. For example, during the war, a man sleeping in a hut on a remote island off northern Scotland suddenly found himself up near the ceiling, looking down at himself lying in bed. He was puzzled but not frightened; the room was filled with a beautiful golden light and in the doorway stood an old friend who was missing after an air-raid over Germany. He was wearing his best Air Force uniform, and said: 'I am quite all right, Johnny.' Next morning the witness awoke with a clear memory of what had happened, and the same day received a letter telling him that his friend was dead.

Other people have reported leaving their body and travelling down a long tunnel towards a bright light at the far end. Some even say that they have entered into a beautiful landscape or seen a gate which they believed to be the entrance to heaven. Some people have sensed a presence or seen people in this beautiful world – but all those who have described such an experience are the ones who had a strong will to live and managed to get back to our world. Such experiences are known as near-death experiences, or NDEs.

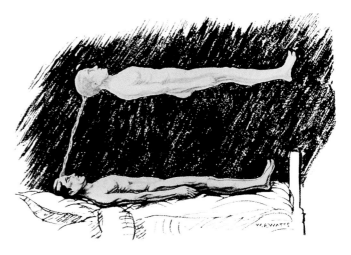

It is believed that the two bodies are joined by a cord during an OBE.

An out-of-body experience depicted using double-exposure photography.

THIS TUNNEL OF TREES was drawn by Dr Susan Blackmore, whose own OBE in 1970 led her to research the subject. She was tired and listening to music when she felt herself travelling at speed along a tree-lined avenue. A friend asked where she was, and she answered: 'I'm on the ceiling.' She could see her body below, with its mouth opening and closing. She saw a 'string or cord, silvery, faintly glowing and moving gently' running between the neck of her physical body and the navel area of her astral body. She imagined that she moved out of the room and flew above the rooftops, visiting Paris, New York and South America, the whole experience lasting three hours. The results of her investigations into OBEs can be read in her book *Beyond the Body* (1982).

RELIGIOUS PHENOMENA

VISIONS

OVER THE CENTURIES, hundreds of people have claimed to have seen a religious vision (usually of the Blessed Virgin Mary) and some of these claims have had far-reaching effects. In 1858, 14-year-old Bernadette Soubirous had a vision of the Virgin Mary in a cave at Lourdes, in southern France, and a healing spring began to flow at the site; today Lourdes is a major healing centre and is visited by people from all over the world.

Many other places where visions have been reported have also become centres of pilgrimage, probably the largest being Fatima in Portugal, where in 1917 three shepherd children saw Our Lady several times and received prophecies from her. As news spread of the visions, crowds came to Fatima, culminating in the events of 13 October, when about 70,000 pilgrims arrived to witness the miracle promised by Our Lady. The weather was wet, but suddenly the clouds parted to reveal the sun, which to many of the pilgrims seemed to be spinning, whirling, and dancing. Blood-red streamers of flame were seen and coloured lights – the sun appeared to plunge to earth before resuming its normal place in the sky – and suddenly the weather was dry and sunny. After eight years of investigation, the Church authorities authorized the veneration of Our Lady of the Rosary of Fatima.

The devotional card from Fatima (right) depicts Our Lady appearing to the three shepherd children. It also incorporates a relic: the blue dot is a piece of cloth that has been 'Touched to the Miraculous Statue of Our Lady, the clothing of Jacinta and Francisco [two of the children], and the stone on which the Angel stood'.

Photographs alleging to show the sun spinning at Fatima are in existence, but very few of actual visions have ever been taken.

THE BLACK-AND-WHITE photograph above shows one of the many visions that were seen above the Coptic Orthodox Church of St Mary at Zeitoun, a suburb of Cairo in Egypt, in 1968. Two car mechanics were the first to see what looked like a nun dressed in white standing on the church roof. They thought she was going to jump off and ran to fetch the police and a priest. The crowd that gathered shouted at her not to jump but, to their amazement, the figure disappeared. A week later she was seen again, and she continued to appear from time to time until 1970. Thousands of people, sometimes 250,000 on one night, would gather to see the visions, which lasted sometimes only for a few minutes but at others for several hours. Before she appeared, flashing lights and clouds would gather above the church and luminous bird-like forms would glide around. The vision of Our Lady (for that is who she was assumed to be, although she spoke to no one) would move around the church roof, bowing to the crowds and moving her arms as if in blessing.

As the photograph shows, both the vision and the church were swathed in auras of bluish-white light, and sometimes the light would move down the church walls to engulf the pilgrims below. Many miraculous cures were reported.

Nearly 30 years later, Our Lady has come back to Egypt and during 1997 sightings of her were reported from the Virgin Mary Church in Shentena Al Hagar, a village 44 miles (70km) north of Cairo. In August, flashes of red light and silver doves were seen, then the Virgin Mary in white robes and blue veil. Soon thousands of people were coming to see the vision, which appeared regularly. Some reports described two angels by her side, and said that she blessed the waiting pilgrims. A bishop said: 'I saw her three times. She appeared in very bright circles of light . . . The third time I saw her transforming into a huge silver dove piercing the sky.'

THE OPPORTUNITIES ARE many for photo-graphing such a miraculous event when Our Lady appears so regularly, but strangely few photographs are ever published. The only colour photograph of a vision of which we are aware was obtained by accident! It is a strange story, told by an art-restorer named Károly Ligeti. On 3 September 1989 he was working in the church at Karácsond in Hungary, restoring a picture on the altar. He was standing on scaffolding in order to reach the picture, and he asked someone to photograph him at work. As he turned he noticed a female figure with a halo and surrounded by light, with an infant beside her. He thought that they were the Blessed Virgin Mary and the baby Jesus Christ. Although nobody else in the church saw the vision, it was captured in the photo-graph. Ligeti was very excited by what he had seen; he also felt very emotional, and fearful, and was unable to work for some days afterwards. When he showed people his photograph, to prove to them the truth of what he had seen, they tried to find a logical explanation: perhaps it was a statue in the church that had been lit by the sun, or perhaps it was all a hoax. However, the parish priest supported him, saying that there was no statue in the church that looked like the figures in the vision and also that it was not a sunny day. He also allowed a copy of the photograph to be displayed in the church, which showed that he did not think it was a hoax. Also, if Károly Ligeti had made up his story and faked the photograph, he would surely have chosen to describe a familiar statue of the two figures and not an unusual grouping, as this was. He would probably also have claimed that the Virgin Mary spoke to him and gave him messages, as so many other visionaries have done, because this would have added to the importance of his vision. He did not do these things, however, and the event has had a profound effect upon him. He said that it has given him great strength to face the rest of his life.

Above right: If you look closely at the photograph of the vision you can see Károly Ligeti himself in the shadows at the top. This is the only photograph of a vision which shows both the vision and the person who witnessed it.

Right: This drawing was done by Ligeti and shows the vision as he saw it.

MIRACLE CURES

THE MIRACLE CURES reported by people who have visited the shrine at Lourdes in France were mentioned on p.121, but shrines dedicated to Our Lady of Lourdes were also developed at other places in Europe. One of these was at Oostakker in Belgium and it was there that a miracle cure happened in 1875. The recipient of the cure was Pierre de Rudder (bottom), who in 1867 had his leg broken by a falling tree. Doctors wanted to amputate the leg because it had become infected, but Pierre would not let them. He suffered terrible pain for many years, but always believed that somehow he would be cured. In 1875 his employer arranged for him to go on a pilgrimage to the shrine at Oostakker. Before he did so, he visited a medical specialist who noted that he had an open wound at the top of his leg. It was possible to see inside the wound and the two leg bones were about 1in (3cm) apart. The lower part of the leg could be moved in all directions, even twisted around so that the heel was in front and the toes behind. His leg was still in this condition when he went to the shrine. At the shrine Pierre was in great pain and couldn't walk. Feeling very tired, he sat and prayed. Suddenly he was overcome by emotion and, without realizing what he was doing, he stood up and walked over to the statue of Our Lady of Lourdes. Then he knelt down. When he realized what had happened, he got up and walked around the shrine. His wife saw him and fainted.

When his leg was examined, it was found that the wound had mysteriously healed, the bones had mended and his legs were the same length again. The cure had in fact been instantaneous, something that is considered to be impossible. Back at home, Pierre's son couldn't believe that this man was his father, because he had never seen him without crutches. Pierre had no more problems with his leg and he lived for a further 23 years. A year after his death, his body was exhumed by a doctor and it was found that new bone had grown to heal the fracture.

The legs were amputated and photographed, and the new bone can be seen in the right-hand leg in the photograph on the left, which was taken at that time. The doctor stated that the cure was absolutely inexplicable and the miracle has never been medically explained.

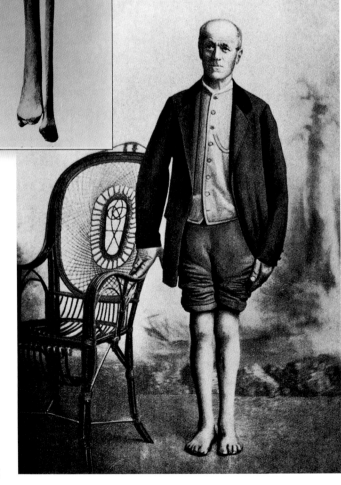

STIGMATA

STIGMATA ARE THE wounds that Christ suffered at his Crucifixion. St Francis of Assisi is the best-known early stigmatic, receiving his stigmata in 1224, just two years before his death. At the time he was on a retreat, living in a hut on the Monte La Verna in Italy and spending his time in prayer and meditation. As he contemplated the Passion of Christ, he saw an angel in the form of a crucified man; it was a vision of Christ. St Francis felt a sense of great joy, sorrow and wonder, and after the vision faded, he found that the marks of the nails he had seen on the vision began to appear on his own hands and feet. He told no one, because of embarrassment, but his companions noticed that he kept his hands and feet covered, and that his clothes were stained with blood. Also he could not walk down from the holy mountain but had to ride on a donkey. The wounds were still visible on his corpse after his death two years later.

There have been several well-attested cases of stigmata during the twentieth century, and many more reported. The case of Thérèse Neumann is well known. Born in Bavaria in 1898, she became an invalid in 1918 and was bedridden. She miraculously recovered some health in 1925 and, that same year, while musing on Jesus's passion, she had a vision:

> All at once I saw the Redeemer before me. I saw him in the Garden of the Mount of Olives . . . Suddenly I felt, while I saw the Saviour, such a pain in my side that I thought: 'Now I am going to die.' At the same time I felt something hot run down my side. It was blood.

She had further visions of the Passion, and wounds opened up in her hands and feet. They began to show on most Fridays and stayed with her for the rest of her life – 36 years. Blood also poured from her eyes.

This photograph, taken during the late 1950s, shows another stigmatic who wept blood, Sister Elena Ajello from Calabria in Italy.

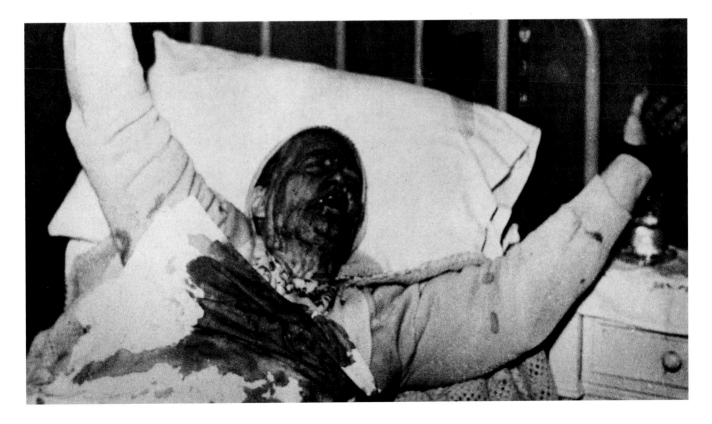

THE PHOTOGRAPHS ON this page show two recent stigmatics, both also from Italy. The hands (right) belong to Antonio Ruffini, who has had the stigmata for 40 years. He built a chapel south of Rome at the place where he saw an apparition of the Blessed Virgin Mary and received the stigmata. The wounds have been examined by doctors. They go through the palms of the hands and the feet; usually such wounds would become infected, but Mr Ruffini has no problem using his hands like a normal person.

THE FEET (below) belong to Giorgio Bongiovanni, who received his stigmata only a few years ago, during a visit to the site of the visions at Fatima. He claims to have visions of Jesus and Mary, who arrive in UFOs. He is part of a UFO cult, which has rented the land and built a centre with a school in an old farmhouse at the place where he had his first vision of Jesus, who descended from a UFO dressed in fuchsia-coloured overalls. His stigmata, in his hands, feet and side, bleed almost daily.

The blood often forms patterns, of the sun or a cross, as shown in the photograph. Bongiovanni has a large following and travels widely to spread his message, which is something like: 'The end is near – the time is ripe for the fulfilling of the Third Secret of Fatima, if the people don't wake up and become aware of their own destructive potential.'

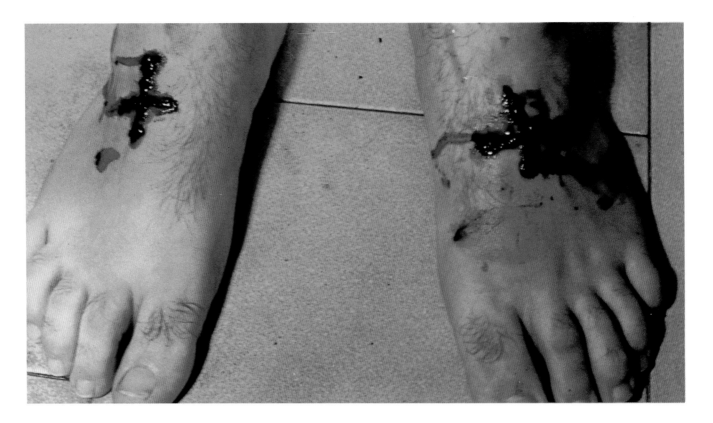

WEEPING AND BLEEDING IMAGES

EVERY YEAR THERE are reports from Catholic communities around the world that religious statues have started to produce tears from their eyes. Sometimes there may be a natural explanation for this apparently mysterious phenomenon: the statues are made of plaster which is porous and can hold water. If the statue is glazed while waterlogged, the water will not be able to escape unless the glaze is scratched. Researchers who are sceptical about the mystery believe that the phenomenon is a hoax and that a hoaxer could carefully scratch away a little of the glaze at the corner of the eyes so that the statue then begins to 'weep'. Although this explanation is superficially convincing, and might explain a few cases, there are plenty of very strange happenings which cannot be so easily explained away. Very often, when the liquid is analysed, it has been found to be indistinguishable from human tears. In one case, the tears vanished when they reached the bottom of the frame in which the weeping portrait of the Virgin Mary was mounted.

In other cases, the tears are of blood. In 1971 a lawyer living in Italy awoke to find that a painting of the Madonna hanging over his bed was dripping blood; it was coming from her eyes, her heart, her hands and her feet, and from the hands and feet of the two saints kneeling beside her. Some of the red liquid was forming crosses on the white wall below the painting. The bleeding continued, even when the police put the painting into a locked box at their headquarters. When analysed, the liquid was found to be human blood, as has also happened in many other cases.

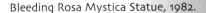

Bleeding Rosa Mystica Statue, 1982.

SOMETIMES THE SUBSTANCE flowing from a religious image is neither tears nor blood, but oil of some kind. A plastic statue of the Virgin Mary in Jordan oozed olive oil in October 1987 whenever it was touched by a ten year-old girl. She would climb onto the table in her home to reach the statue, which stood on a wall unit, and then rub her oily fingers on the hands of the pilgrims who had gathered to see the miracle.

It is possible that there is some kind of link between bleeding images and poltergeist phenomena. Also, people who have the stigmata sometimes find that the religious images in their homes are bleeding as well. These events may be caused by a build-up of powerful emotions, in the same way that strong emotions are thought to be involved in the development of poltergeist phenomena. In 1920, in Ireland, a 16-year-old boy, who was a devout Catholic, found that all his religious images began to bleed and so, too, did the images in another house after he had visited. At the same time, he was the focus of poltergeist disturbances.

Weeping statue of Our Lady of Maasmechelen, Belgium.

INCORRUPTION

THE TERM 'INCORRUPTION' generally refers to a dead body which does not decay after death. There are very many instances of the bodies of holy people being exhumed some time after burial and being found apparently immune to natural decay. Other mysteries associated with the death of a holy person include: unusual fragrances being smelled around the body, persisting for months or years; no rigor mortis, the limbs being as flexible as those of a living person; the bleeding of corpses weeks, months or even years after death; and the persistence of warmth for some hours after death. It was reported that, in 1607, when a surgeon opened the body of Maria Villani nine hours after her death, in order to extract her heart, the heat in her chest cavity was such that he could not keep his hand inside.

Such scarcely believable cases are rare, but reports of incorrupt bodies are well attested and there are many accounts from eyewitnesses. The extract below refers to the body of Mother Mary Margaret of the Angels (Margaret Wake), who died in 1678 and was buried in Antwerp. Her body was accidentally revealed 38 years later, when the crypt was being enlarged. All the other bodies buried there had decayed naturally but, despite the vault being damp, and her clothing being rotted and soaked in moisture, the body was still whole. A surgeon cut into her body and found that the heart, liver, lungs, muscles, etc. were 'perfectly entire'. Father Thomas Hunter SJ reported:

> This holy body appears of a brownish complexion, but full of flesh, which like a living body yields to any impression made upon it, and rises again of itself when it is pressed, the joints flexible. You find a little moisture when you touch the flesh, but this is not so sensible as when the grave was first opened, and this very frequently breathes out an odoriferous balsamic smell, which is not only perceptible to those about the body, but has sometimes filled the whole room. I mentioned before that it had

been observed that blood flowed out of the grave [more precisely, a horizontal stone niche in the crypt] after the body had been deposited in it. This happened about six weeks after her death, and when her body was found incorrupt, they all took notice that both the sides and lid of the coffin seemed all to be tinged with blood.

Sometimes when the bodies of non-devout people are accidentally disinterred they have been found to be incorrupt, as in a case from Northumberland, UK, probably dating from around the middle of the last century. Some students were helping to dig a grave in the churchyard at Haydon Bridge and at a depth of around 3ft (90cm) they unexpectedly found a coffin. Removing the lid, and pulling away the linen sheet, they found inside it:

> . . . the body of a young 'lass' . . . [who] looked as if she had just fallen asleep. Her eyes were closed, and both her face, which was very beautiful, even in death, and her hands, which were crossed over her breast, were as if they were moulded of pure wax. Her hair was silky and golden, and flashed in the morning sunlight.

The sexton replaced the linen and covered the whole with sacking. When the rector was brought, later in the day, and the sacking removed, they saw that:

> . . . of the beautiful girl whom we had gazed upon only a few hours before, there now only remained a skeleton. The face, the hands, the hair, aye, the very linen itself, everything, everything, had disappeared, and left no more than a disordered heap of what one calls dust.

It has usually been the case, when the bodies of saints and other saintly people have been exhumed, that they have remained incorrupt, despite exposure to the air.

FATHER PAUL OF MOLL

The exhumation shown in the photograph below took place in July 1899 at the cemetery of Termonde in Belgium, and the corpse visible inside the coffin is that of the Very Reverend Father Paul of Moll, Flemish Benedictine and wonder-worker, who had died in February 1896, aged 72. The corpse was in a perfect state of preservation, as was attested to by 22 witnesses of the exhumation. They declared that:

> . . . the skin of the face was hardened and of a
> bister [brownish] colour, the hands very white. His
> monastic habit was clean, and the body had preserved
> its original position notwithstanding the fact that
> the coffin had been dragged up almost perpendicularly
> from the tomb, from a depth of four metres [12ft].

THE SHROUD OF TURIN

CONTROVERSY CONTINUES TO rage around a piece of linen which, for centuries, has been venerated as the shroud which covered Jesus Christ at his burial. Not surprisingly, it has proved difficult to trace the history of the shroud right back to the time of Christ and this has led to claims of forgery. A recent attempt to prove conclusively whether or not the shroud was genuine, by using radio-carbon dating, has not given the clear-cut answer so greatly desired by all parties. The result, announced late in 1988, was that the flax from which the shroud was woven had been harvested between 1260 and 1390 - and the sceptics breathed a sigh of relief. The Turin Shroud was branded a forgery by the media and everyone who had been discomfited by its existence thought it would be forgotten, joining all the other impossible relics which have been proffered as the genuine article: the nails from the true cross (29 of which are claimed to exist), the phials of Christ's blood collected at the Crucifixion; the holy tears of Christ; Christ's navel, saved by the Virgin Mary after his birth and carefully guarded by her; even Christ's foreskin, of which at least eight are said to exist; and drops of the Virgin Mary's milk (69 locations have been traced). The Holy Shroud of Turin, however, could not be so easily dismissed and many experts have been unable to accept the carbon dating. Experts on medieval painting, for instance, say that a fourteenth-century date for this painting (if it were proved to be a painting) would create more problems than if the shroud were found to be genuine! Numerous people have expressed doubts about the validity of the carbon dating and the mystery remains unsolved.

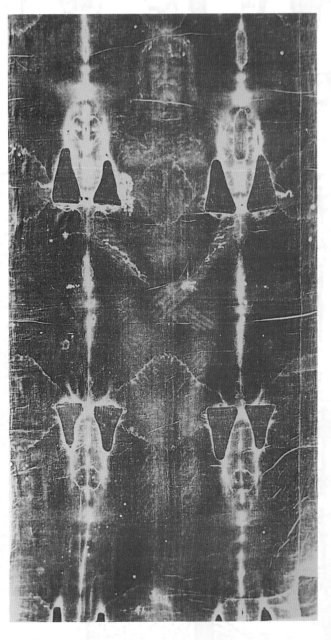

WEIRD
HAPPENINGS

INTRODUCTION

A WIDE VARIETY of mysteries – mystery animals, ghosts and spirits, and strange powers – has been covered in the previous sections, and this final section covers miscellaneous mysteries which don't fit easily into any of these sections. They are no less interesting for being miscellaneous, however, and they can all be classed together under the umbrella heading of 'Fortean phenomena'. That word 'Fortean' might be a bit puzzling. What precisely does it mean? In fact it comes from a name, and commemorates Charles Hoy Fort.

Fort was a collector of weird facts at a time when it was not a normal thing to do. Born in 1874, in New York State, USA, he lived his early life in New York City, spending much of his time in the New York Public Library. He later moved to London, UK, for a while and continued his researches in the British Museum Reading Room. For 27 years he read through the files of scientific magazines and journals and newspapers, carefully noting by hand (this was before the days of the photocopier) all the weird stories which he found. He accumulated many shoeboxes full of slips of paper, which he used to write his four published books: *The Book of the*

Damned, New Lands, Lo! and *Wild Talents*. His writing style is not easy to read and he expresses some unusual ideas, often contrary to conventional wisdom. Here, for instance, are his thoughts on early humans:

> Possibly the remote ancestors of human beings were apes, though no evolutionist has made clear to me reasons for doubting the equally plausible theory that apes have either ascended, or descended, from humans. Still, I think that humans may have evolved from apes, because the simians openly imitate humans, as if conscious of a higher state, whereas the humans who act like apes are likely to deny it when criticized.

He also had a gentle sense of humour, as his thoughts on life reveal:

> Is life worth living? Like everybody else, I have many times asked that question, usually deciding negatively, because I am most likely to ask myself whether life is worth living at times when I am convinced it isn't. One day, in one of my frequent, and probably incurable, scientific moments, it occurred to me to find out. For a month, at the end of each day, I set down a plus sign, or a minus sign, indicating that, in my opinion, life had, or had not, been worth living, that day. At the end of the month, I totalled up, and I can't say that I was altogether pleased to learn that the pluses had won the game. It is not dignified to be optimistic.

Charles Hoy Fort died in 1932, aged 58, a year after the Fortean Society was launched in the USA. Later, in 1965, the International Fortean Organization (INFO) was formed, and this still exists and publishes a regular journal. The organization can also supply a one-volume (1,125-page) edition of the works of Charles Fort. In 1973 another, now well-known, publication came quietly into existence. Published by Bob Rickard, a long-time fan of Charles Fort, it was then called simply *The News*, but soon changed its name to *Fortean Times*. The same company also publishes an annual collection of serious papers under the name *Fortean Studies,* and has recently issued new editions of Charles Fort's books. Only a few years after *Fortean Times* came into existence, we began to collect illustrations on a Fortean theme, and so the Fortean Picture Library was born. (See p.172 for details of how all these organizations may be contacted.)

The range of subjects covered by Fortean researchers is very wide: if it is strange, it is relevant. The coverage of this book is some indication of the scope of Forteana. Here, in this final section, can be found such items as the Dover Demon, Mothman and other non-human creatures, abduction by aliens, fairies and the 'little people', strange rains (ice, frogs, fish, etc.), ball lightning and other mystery lights, spontaneous human combustion, crop circles,

unexpected faces and, to conclude, a few examples of things that might at first glance seem mysterious but really aren't. We hope that our selection of mysteries has whetted your appetite and will make you want to delve deeper into strange phenomena. (See p.172 for a list of recommended books and magazines.)

NON-HUMANS

There are many reports world-wide from people who claim to have seen living beings which are clearly not human. Fairies come into this category, as do UFO entities, or aliens, and winged people; and there are also some creatures with both human and animal features. Are all these beings 'real', as we understand the term, or are they imaginary? Are they simply misidentifications of 'normal' creatures, or are they something beyond scientific understanding, perhaps from another reality?

DOVER DEMON

THE CREATURE THAT became known as the Dover Demon has never been identified. It was 3 or 4ft (0.9 or 1.2m) tall and had a thin body, with long, thin arms and legs, and long fingers and toes. Its large head was shaped like a watermelon and sat on a thin neck. No nose or mouth were seen, but it had large eyes which shone like 'two orange marbles'. Apparently hairless, the creature had a rough, peach-coloured skin. The same description was given by all those who saw the creature: all were sensible teenagers living in Dover, Massachusetts, USA.

The time was April 1977 and three friends were driving one night along a road bordered by trees, fields and widely spaced houses. Suddenly the car headlights picked up a strange creature which 17-year-old Bill Bartlett at first thought was a cat or dog moving along a low stone wall. As he looked at it, he realized it definitely wasn't a cat or dog! He was about 20ft (6m) away from it, and his sighting lasted for five or six seconds. Being an amateur artist, he could clearly remember what he had seen and made a drawing of it as soon as he got home. Unfortunately the two friends with him in the car saw nothing. When Bill told them, they wanted to turn around and go back to look for it, but Bill refused, saying: 'When you see something like that, you don't want to stand around and see what it's going to do.' However, after a short while, he did agree to drive back but they saw nothing.

Meanwhile, 15-year-old John Baxter was walking home just over a mile (1.6km) away from the Bartlett sighting, when he saw someone walking towards him on the same side of the road. He couldn't see any detail because it was very dark, but he thought it might be a kid he knew. He called out, but there was no answer. When it was about 25ft (8m) away, the figure stopped, then ran off down a wooded gully. John followed and saw it standing about 30ft (9m) away, with its long fingers grasping a tree trunk and its toes curled around a

John Baxter with his drawing of the Dover Demon.

136

rock. Like Bill he also saw two light-coloured eyes, but no other facial details. Feeling nervous, he went back to the road and walked quickly home, where he drew a sketch. Later, when he heard about Bill's sighting, they compared drawings and realized they had both seen the same creature.

A day later, 18-year-old Will Taintor and 15-year-old Abby Brabham saw the 'demon' while driving in the same area. It was crouched on all fours beside the road and they were only 8ft (2.4m) away from it as they drove past. They saw its large head, hairless, beige-coloured body and round, glowing, bright green eyes. Apart from this different eye colour, the

A painting of the Dover Demon by Bill Bartlett.

description is exactly the same as those of Bill and John.

All the teenagers were frightened by what they saw and all agreed that the creature was not something they recognized. Did it perhaps come from another world, a parallel universe whose door opened briefly to allow this alien being to wander into our strange world? Maybe it was lost and afraid, wondering how to get back home. We shall never know, for it has never been seen again.

MOTHMAN

FROM TIME TO TIME, giant birds and birdmen have been seen in the USA, but the most terrifying winged creature of recent times must be the one that became known as Mothman.

Its first recorded appearance seems to have been in 1960 or 1961, close to the Ohio River in West Virginia. A woman was driving with her father when they saw a tall, man-like figure standing on the road. She described what happened:

> I slowed down and as we got closer we could see that it was much larger than a man. A big grey figure. It stood in the middle of the road. Then a pair of wings unfolded from its back and they practically filled the whole road. It almost looked like a small airplane. Then it took off straight up . . . disappearing out of sight in seconds. We were both terrified. I stepped on the gas and raced out of there. We talked it over and decided not to tell anybody about it. Who would believe us anyway?

A few years later, the same creature, or one very similar, was causing panic in the vicinity of a World War Two ammunition dump near Point Pleasant, also in West Virginia. These were the events that gave rise to the name Mothman. One of the earliest of the frightening confrontations took place in November 1966 around midnight when two young couples were driving along a dirt road by an abandoned power plant. They saw a grey figure, as tall as a man, with wings and glowing red eyes, shuffling towards the door of the plant. As they drove quickly away, at times reaching 100 mph (160km/h), the creature appeared overhead and kept up with them without flapping its wings.

The very next day, a woman visiting friends in the area was getting out of her car when she saw a grey figure with red eyes which seemed to rise out of the ground. It was staring at her and she stood as if paralysed while the friends with her ran for the house. Somehow she picked up her young daughter, who she had dropped in her terror, and got safely into the house. Many other sightings were made in November and December and, when all the witnesses' reports were compared, a clearer picture of Mothman emerged. It was 5–7ft (1.5–2.1m) tall, broader than a man, with legs like a man's, although its feet were never seen, and it appeared to have no arms. It had luminous, bright red eyes which were apparently set into its shoulders, as no one had seen a head. Its wings extended to about 10ft (3m), and were folded against its back when not in use. They did not flap when it was flying and it could move very fast, over 100 mph (160km/h). It was never heard to speak but some witnesses heard a mouse-like squeaking noise coming from it.

Although the creature became known as Mothman, it was clearly not a human being – but what was it? At the time when it was being seen in West Virginia, there were also a lot of UFO sightings, so could the two be linked? Was it some kind of alien creature, or even a robot? Unfortunately none of the witnesses stayed around long enough to talk to it, or to take its photograph, so we shall never know whether it really existed or was merely a figment of some over-active imaginations.

UFO ENTITIES AND ALIENS

Over the past 50 years, there have been thousands of reports of strange flying craft seen around the world. At first they were called 'flying saucers', then 'unidentified flying objects', or UFOs. Since, despite the rumours, none of these craft has ever been captured, and there are no photographs that are known to be 100 per cent reliable, it might be that all the reports are either hoaxes or misidentifications of normal astronomical events or terrestrial objects.

ONE VIEWPOINT AT the other extreme is that UFOs are craft from other worlds outside our solar system, or from other dimensions or parallel universes. According to this scenario, these craft carry beings from other worlds, who are usually described as humanoid in appearance, although often with some non-human features, such as large wrap-around eyes or green skin. Many types of entity have been reported but, in recent years, the description has become standardized: the aliens are short in stature, with large heads and spindly bodies, large, wrap-around eyes, and an insatiable curiosity about the human body, which leads them to abduct humans by the thousand and subject them to frightening physical examinations.

A classic case of this kind took place in November 1975 and the victim (or abductee, as they are often known) was Travis Walton, who was working with six other men in the Apache–Sitgreaves National Forest in Arizona, USA. They were using chainsaws to thin out the trees and on 5 November they had worked all day in the forest, as usual. At sundown they got into their truck to drive back home to Snowflake and were driving through the forest when they saw a golden light shining among the trees. It came from a disc-shaped object hovering in the air and they stopped the truck to get a better look at it. Travis jumped out and ran up the hillside towards it, while the others shouted at him to come back. He said afterwards:

> I hadn't planned to go any closer, but just as I
> raised up from a crouching position to move
> away, the thing began to move and made
> sounds, a combination of high-pitched sounds
> with some low components, and then I felt like
> I was hit over the head and at the same time I
> felt kind of an electric shock throughout my
> whole body and that's all I can remember.

Travis Walton photographed ten years after the abduction.

The UFO entity that Travis Walton saw, drawn from Walton's description by his boss Michael Rogers.

What the other men saw was a bluish-green ray come from the craft, striking Travis in the head and chest, so that he fell backwards with his arms outstretched. They panicked and drove off at speed but, when they saw a light streaking away, they reckoned that the UFO had gone and decided to return to look for Travis. Arriving back in the clearing, they soon saw that he had gone and, even though they searched with flashlights, there was no trace of him. Very upset, they went home and reported the disappearance to the sheriff.

In the following days, many people searched for the missing man, but no trace was found. Suspicion fell on his workmates, who took lie-detector tests to prove that they had not murdered him. Then, after five days, when everyone was losing hope, Travis's sister received a phone call from him. He was found at a filling station near Heber, several miles from home, in a weak and thirsty state. He was also mentally confused, and very surprised to learn that he had been gone for five days; he thought it was only a couple of hours!

When he had recovered, he described what had happened to him. After being zapped by the blue light, he had woken up to find himself on a table in a white room, which he naturally thought was some kind of hospital. He knew something strange was happening when he saw three creatures about 5ft (1.5m) tall standing by the table. They had round, domed heads, large eyes and small noses, mouths and ears. He also noted that they seemed to have no fingernails. They all wore strange-coloured, one-piece garments. Travis threw onto the floor an oval, silvery object that was lying on his chest, then jumped up, following the three creatures who were leaving the room. Outside were corridors, so he followed one that led away from the direction the creatures had taken. He wandered about and explored empty rooms; then a man 6ft (1.8m) tall and wearing a helmet over his head, and looking like a normal human being, came in and motioned for Travis to go with him. Travis asked lots of questions, which the man ignored. On the way they passed through a large area where there were craft like the one he saw in the forest. When they reached another room, Travis was left with three other human-looking people who indicated that he should climb up on a table. They placed a mask on his face and he became unconscious. He woke up to find himself lying on a pavement with a huge UFO close by. After it shot away, he got up and walked for a while to try to find out where he was. He realized he was at Heber and made a phone call to his sister.

In the years that followed, countless researchers have tried to find a solution to the mystery of what actually happened to Travis Walton. Some people think it was all a hoax, but nothing can be proved and Travis and his colleagues insist that it all happened just as they described.

FAIRIES AND THE LITTLE PEOPLE

Fairies do not live only in the pages of books: many people claim to have seen them in real life. The meetings are usually short-lived and always unexpected, and quite often the witnesses are children.

AN ALLEGED ENCOUNTER with fairies took place 100 years ago, on the rocky moorland of Dartmoor in Devon. The 'pixy' seen by a little girl was 'like a little wizened man . . . eighteen inches [45cm] or possibly two feet [60cm] high. It had a little pointed hat . . . a doublet, and little short knickers . . . Its face was brown and wrinkled and wizened. I saw it for a moment, and it vanished. It was under a boulder when I looked, and then vanished.' This is a typical description of real live fairies – they very rarely have wings, nor are they wearing pretty clothes. Those are the fairies of fairy tales and also the fairies which appear in hoaxed photographs.

One famous set of hoaxed fairy photographs is known as the 'Cottingley fairies', after the place in Yorkshire, UK, where the fairies were supposedly seen early this century. Two young girls claimed to

Frances Griffiths in one of the famous 'Cottingley fairy' photographs of dancing fairies, July 1917.

Elsie Wright with a gnome, September 1917.

have seen fairies by the stream near their home, but nobody would believe them, so they decided to take photographs to prove that the fairies really did exist. The five photographs they produced convinced many people of the reality of fairies – until a few years ago, when it was proved that the fairies were really cut-out figures which one of the girls had drawn. By now elderly ladies, Frances Griffiths and Elsie Wright admitted that they had made the fairies and had taken the photographs. Two of the photographs in question, which were taken in 1917, appear here.

A FAIRY GLEN

Sometimes an encounter with fairies can be very subtle, as happened to John L. Hall in 1994, while he was walking through Glen Aldyn on the Isle of Man, UK. The island is traditionally a fairy-haunted place, something John was very aware of, as he was a regular visitor, searching out the atmospheric places. As he and his companion walked through the wooded valley, they heard what sounded like drumming, music and tinkling voices. Was it simply the water rushing over the rocky stream-bed, they wondered? At one point the path was full of water and they had to detour through dark, overhanging trees. John began to feel strange, as though they were being watched, and he said that they should turn back. He felt sick and looked very pale; his vision was fuzzy and he felt as though his back was wrapped in 'a cold wet clammy blanket'. He turned and photographed the trees they had just passed through before retracing their steps along the path. Later, when he saw the photographs he had taken, he found that the first one showed what looked like 'a strange looking green man on a pedestal' in the tree foliage. Both John and his companion were affected by the strange atmosphere in the glen. The girl he was with saw a strange mist and heard 'music like someone or something playing drums and flutes playing soft music'. Did their imaginations play tricks with them both, or did they momentarily step into fairyland?

The photograph that John took (shown below) tantalizes: does it really show a fairy - or merely patterns in the leaves and branches?

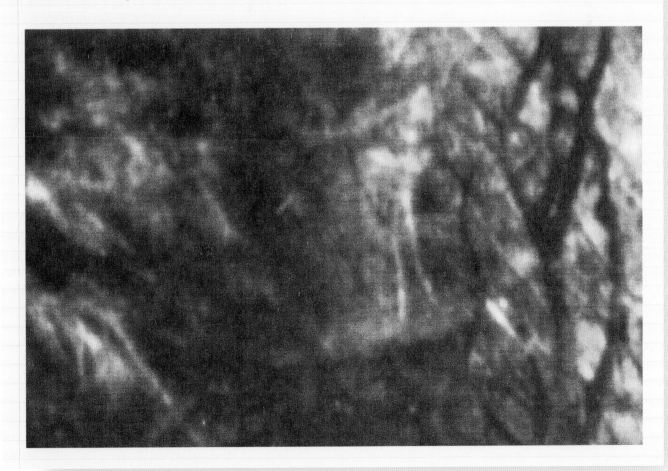

REAL FAIRIES SEEM to enjoy dancing and are often engaged in that pursuit when seen by humans. Usually the human witness is alone when he/she comes across a group of dancing fairies in some lonely country spot. It used to be believed that, if you saw them dancing and decided to join in, you would not be able to leave the circle but would have to stay with the fairies for many years. However, 50 years of human time would seem like only a few minutes if you were with the fairies and, in folklore, there are tales of people returning from what they thought was a short visit to fairyland, only to discover that all the people they knew had grown old and died.

This reminds us of the UFO abduction case (p.139), in which Travis Walton was away from home for five days but thought it had only been a couple of hours. Also, UFO entities are almost always small, like the little people, and it has been suggested that the UFO abduction experience is the modern version of being kidnapped by fairies.

People who claim to see fairies sometimes describe miniature vehicles, like the little red and white cars used by the 60 fairies seen by a group of children in Nottingham, UK, in 1979. The children heard a tinkly bell and saw the little men in cars coming out of the bushes. They had greenish, crinkly faces and long white beards. They were driving around laughing but the children were frightened and ran away. Forty years earlier, three children asleep at home in Cornwall, UK, awoke to hear strange noises – a buzzing, music and bells – and when they looked out of the window they saw a tiny red car being driven around the yard by a little man with a white beard and a 'red droopy pointed hat'. He also looked very happy. A few years earlier, two young children had seen a tiny aeroplane with a wingspan of 12–15in (30–37cm) land in their garden briefly, before flying away again. The tiny pilot wore a leather flying-helmet and waved at the children as he took off. Also in the early years of this century, two children in the remote Scottish islands saw a fairy boat and talked to two tiny boys dressed in green. A tiny woman on the boat gave them some loaves of bread the size of walnuts and invited them aboard, but they refused the offer.

There is not much physical evidence to support the existence of fairies. A few tiny artefacts have been found, such as the 3in (7.5cm) long fairy shoe found in Ireland in 1835, tiny clay pipes and utensils, tiny arrowheads – all, naturally enough, attributed to the fairies. Occasionally the buried remains of dwarf human beings are found, like the mummified body (left) that was discovered in the Pedro Mountains of Wyoming, USA, in October 1932 by prospectors searching for gold. It was said to be sitting on a rock ledge in a cave. Its height in a sitting position was 6½in (16.5cm); it would have been 14in (35.5cm) tall if standing. Was it a representative of a pygmy Indian tribe who once lived in the mountains or was it merely a mummified child? Opinions differ. This, however, is not the only evidence for a pygmy race, for small skulls have been found in the USA, not only in Wyoming but also in Montana's Beartooth Mountains.

Mummified dwarf found in Wyoming, USA in 1932.

STRANGE RAINS

A frog-fall, as illustrated on the cover of *Fate* magazine in 1958.

RAIN, HAIL, SNOW and meteorites are not the only things to fall from the sky! 'Ice-bombs' are regularly reported – such as the 100lb (45.4kg) block which fell through Edith Turner's roof in Florida, USA, in July 1982. It is true that sometimes these unwelcome arrivals are deposited by passing planes, the ice often being frozen toilet-waste. This is not always true, however, as ice falls when no planes are in the area and, indeed, in this particular case it fell before planes were invented. According to one theory, the earth's oceans contain water that originally came from comets made of ice, which bombarded the earth millions of years ago, and the water level is still being topped up by small ice-comets.

Next in frequency of reports are falls of fishes, frogs and toads. Some scientists doubt that these creatures fall from the sky and they say that, if someone sees hundreds of frogs on the ground during a heavy rain-shower, it is simply that the welcome rain must have brought the creatures out of cover. However, people have reported *seeing* frogs and fishes falling, and hitting their umbrellas. The animals are often alive when they land, so clearly they haven't been in the sky for very long. The most sensible scientific explanation is that they were caught up from their pond by a whirlwind or water-spout, which then dropped them again not too far away. However, often no unusual winds or violent weather are reported in the area and there are numerous reports of creatures falling from clear skies, on still days, and of repeated falls in the same place.

Even stranger are reports of falls of blood, and even flesh, for example the strips of flesh with blood and hairs which fell on a town in California, USA, in 1869, or the flakes of meat drifting down from a clear sky over Kentucky, USA, in 1876. Eggs fell on schoolchildren at Wokingham in Berkshire, UK, in 1974, peas and beans have fallen in various places, and rice fell on parts of Burma in 1952. Solid objects and mystery liquids have also crashed or floated downwards, but the most welcome arrival must surely be coins and paper money.

Thousands of 1,000-franc notes fluttered down on Bourges, France, in 1957, while a French two-franc piece, fell into a garden in North Carolina, USA, in October 1958. Mr and Mrs McGee were in the garden when it fell, but could see no plane from which it might have dropped. In December 1975, dollar bills fell into a Chicago street and $588 were collected and handed in to the police, while in Germany, in January 1976, two clergymen gathered up 2,000 marks in paper money which they saw falling from a clear sky.

Although there are scientific explanations for some of these events, there are many reports which stretch the imagination. Charles Fort (see pp.134–5) thought that there must be a 'Super-Sargasso Sea' somewhere up above us where all kinds of creatures and objects from earth are gathered together, some of them occasionally being sprinkled onto us as a kind of supernatural practical joke. He may have been right!

Fish that fell from the sky over East Ham, London, UK, in May 1984. They were among six fish found on the roof of a house and may have fallen during a heavy rainstorm in the night. Other falls were reported not far away.

BALLS OF LIGHT

BALL LIGHTNING

SMALL BALLS OF LIGHT, moving fast through the air, sometimes buzzing or hissing, sometimes smelling of sulphur, are as frightening as they sound, and they are also unexplained. They can vary in size from 1in to 5ft (2.5cm to 1.5m) in diameter and their colour varies from yellow to red, bluish white, or even purple or green. They can exist for anything from a few seconds to ten minutes or more, and they either simply disappear or explode. They can travel freely, sometimes against the wind, and they can even enter houses.

Ball lightning is not especially rare; there are hundreds of good and reliable reports on record, many of them made by scientists. Nevertheless, no one has yet been able to explain what ball lightning is and how it comes into existence. It can be destructive to property and can also cause injury to people with whom it comes into contact, but the smaller balls seem to be less harmful. They enter houses and 'explore', as if they are intelligent. In 1961, during a thunderstorm, a woman in a house in England noticed a fireball in the room. Frightened, she ran upstairs and it followed her, passing her on the stairs before shooting out of a bedroom window with a loud crash like thunder.

Ball lightning also enters houses through open windows – and through keyholes, under doors and down chimneys. In 1952, in Germany, again during a storm, a gleaming purplish sphere was seen outside a closed window and then it was in the room, so it must have somehow passed through the glass. Ball lightning seen inside aircraft must also have passed through a solid surface.

From time to time, people have been knocked unconscious by being in contact with an exploding fireball. Two men sheltering inside a log barn in Canada during a storm in 1925 saw a fireball come in at the door and hit the end of the log on which one of them was sitting. It then circled around inside before knocking a hole in the end wall and disappearing. The man sitting on the log remained unconscious for eight hours; the other man was thrown 15ft (4.5m) into the field. Even more horrible was the encounter with a fireball reported by five mountaineers in the Caucasus Mountains in 1978. One man woke up to see a bright yellow blob floating inside the tent. It disappeared into his friend's sleeping-bag and the man screamed in pain. It came out and moved from bag to bag, causing extreme pain to whoever it touched. One man was killed and the man who reported the events was knocked unconscious several times. In hospital seven wounds were found on his body. They were worse than burns, with pieces of muscle torn out to the bone, and his companions had suffered in the same way.

Although it seems unlikely that a ball of light can show signs of intelligence, there are some strange cases on record which should be carefully considered. In 1921 a priest living in Pennsylvania, USA, reported that he was in the bathroom during a thunderstorm. A yellow, grapefruit-sized ball of light came in through the open window and rolled around his feet. Then it 'hopped up' into the washbasin and melted the steel chain before disappearing. Several weeks later, the same man was standing in the same bathroom during another storm – and exactly the same thing occurred. A ball of fire came into the room, circled his feet and then hopped into the bathtub (as a change from the washbasin!) and melted the steel chain holding the rubber plug.

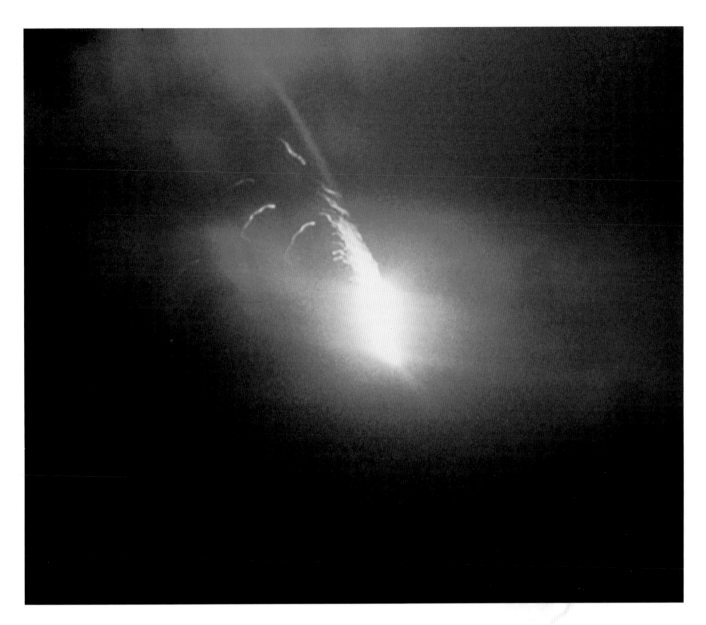

THIS PHOTOGRAPH SHOWING possible ball lightning was taken by Werner Burger at his home in Sankt Gallenkirch, Vorarlberg, Austria. One summer night in 1978 he was watching an approaching storm and put his camera on a tripod and went out onto the balcony to photograph lightning flashes. While taking time exposures, he heard a strange noise, like a sparkler or the rasp of a wire brush, and saw a fireball drop. He released the shutter and caught the event on film. Investigators have ruled out a meteor, fireworks or ordinary lightning, and it is interesting that about 17 more ball lightning reports have been recorded from the immediate vicinity at various times.

MYSTERY LIGHTS

STRANGE NIGHT-TIME LIGHTS are sometimes seen that fall into no known category of phenomena. They are not up in the sky but at low level, and they may be very small, like a golf ball in size. One such event took place in 1952, in the English Midlands near Coventry, when someone out for an evening stroll saw 'a number of bubbles', golf-ball size, moving in the opposite direction to the breeze. They circled around him, as if exploring him, before joining to form a 'goldfish bowl, dirty inside the glass' and then disappearing.

Some of these lights have become a regular feature at certain locations, where they are known as 'ghost lights' or 'spook lights'.

THE PHOTOGRAPH BELOW shows the mysterious Marfa lights in Texas, USA. It was taken in September 1986 by James Crocker. Some lights of this kind have been found to be caused by distant car headlights seen through shimmering air, or by refractions of artificial lights, but not all can be explained in this way. Local people sometimes have their own explanations, often involving the ghost of a dead railway man carrying a lantern.

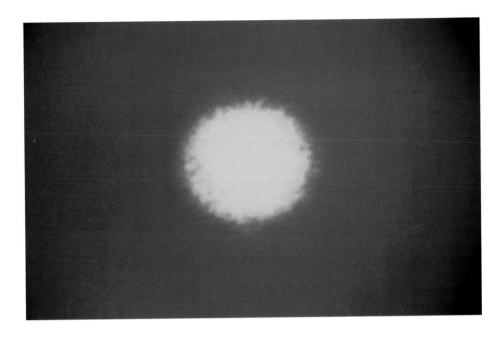

LUMINOUS LIGHT BALL

If a mystery light is large enough, it might be seen as a UFO. This happened in southern France in November 1974, when 16-year-old Christophe Fernandez was preparing for an evening visit to the nearby town of Uzès. While closing the shutters, he noticed a luminous ball on the ground about 40yd (37m) away, motionless despite the strong wind. At times it seemed to be transparent and he could then see the dry-stone wall through it. He watched it for 10-15 minutes, then remembered his camera. He approached to within 25yd (23m) of the light before taking pictures of it (right). He heard a regular sound, like a bottle emptying, and saw three circular patches of a deeper colour moving around on the light. As he continued to watch,

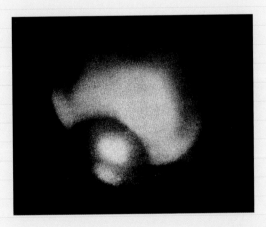

the globe rose a few yards into the air and a 'cylinder' emerged from underneath it. Then the light shot upwards and disappeared in a fraction of a second. When Christophe passed the place where the light had been, he noticed a feeling of warmth. Investigators found nothing unusual at the site. However, a dowsing rod reacted strongly and Christophe's father confirmed that there was a strong underground flow of water along a line linking the location of the light with the house. It is likely that this link is not just a coincidence and that, rather than being an alien craft, the light was in fact some kind of natural phenomenon, although such an explanation does not explain the cylinder which Christophe claimed he had seen.

SPONTANEOUS FIRES

Fires that light up with no one being present are fortunately rare, but there are some strange cases of spontaneous fires on record.

SOMETIMES HOUSES ARE plagued by mysterious outbreaks of fire and these are thought to be somehow linked with poltergeist phenomena. These 'noisy ghosts' are responsible for creating fear and chaos in households, throwing objects around, making things disappear and then reappear, etc. When they add fire-raising to their repertoire, the experience becomes truly frightening. (See also p.79.)

Fortunately, mysterious fires in houses are just a nuisance and do not usually result in injury to the people who live there. However, some victims have experienced their clothing, and also their bedclothes, bursting into flames, and in 1975 an Indian lady, Shanti, was burned to death in such a case. Her house in Lucknow in India had been the focus of inexplicable phenomena, including the burning of clothes and bedding, and one day Shanti was set alight in bed and died of her injuries.

A number of other sad cases are on record in which people have apparently burst into flames and either been badly injured or even burned to death.

This phenomenon is known as 'spontaneous human combustion' and one strange aspect of it is that some victims have been found in their homes so badly burned that only a small part of the body was recognizable. In 1951, elderly widow Mrs Mary Hardy Reeser was reduced to a pile of ashes in her St Petersburg home in Florida, USA. Only a foot in a slipper and a shrunken skull were found – but even though a very high temperature is needed to reduce a body to ashes, items only 5ft (1.5m) away from the armchair where she died were untouched by the blaze. The photographs show Mrs Reeser as she was when alive (below right) and also the official clean-up after her strange death (below left).

IN THE CASE of Dr John Irving Bentley, who died at Coudersport, Pennsylvania, USA, on 5 December 1966, all that remained after the mystery blaze was his lower leg and foot in a slipper (see the photograph above). A hole had been burned in his bathroom floor and a pile of ashes was found in the basement below, but there were no other remains of the unfortunate doctor.

CROP CIRCLES

Crop circles are a modern mystery, having been first recorded in the UK c.1980. Throughout the 1980s, simple circles would appear in the summer corn in Wiltshire and Hampshire, and investigators sought a natural explanation.

THE PHOTORAPH ON the right shows a simple circle which appeared on the night of 13/14 August 1986 in the corn at the Devil's Punchbowl, Cheesefoot Head, Hampshire, a popular site for the phenomenon. Whirlwinds were at first thought to be responsible, but it seems unlikely that an unstable whirlwind could form precisely outlined circles, sometimes with an outer ring, or with four separate circles arranged around it. Therefore the researchers looked for some other natural explanation and the idea of the plasma vortex was born, whereby a miniature whirlwind was formed in specific atmospheric conditions. This theory was supported by a few people who claimed to have seen crop circles forming. In Scotland in August 1989, Sandy Reid watched from 49ft (15m) away as a localized wind rustled the corn and a 'force' shot downwards and a circle appeared instantaneously.

Below: a whirlwind on Beckhampton Down, Wiltshire, in July 1989.

CROP CIRCLE EYEWITNESSES

In May 1990 in Surrey, UK, Vivienne and Gary Tomlinson pictured below also saw a crop circle form and described it as follows:

We were standing on a narrow footpath at the edge of a cornfield, when we saw the corn on our right was moving. There was a mist hovering above and we heard a high-pitched sound. Then we felt a strong wind pushing us from the side and above. It was forcing down on our heads so that we could hardly stay upright yet my husband's hair was standing on end. It was incredible. Then the whirling air seemed to branch into two and zigzagged off into the distance. We could still see it like a light mist or fog, shimmering as it moved. As it disappeared we were left standing in the circle with the corn flattened all around us. Everything became very still again and we were left with a tingly feeling. It all happened so quickly it seemed like a split second.

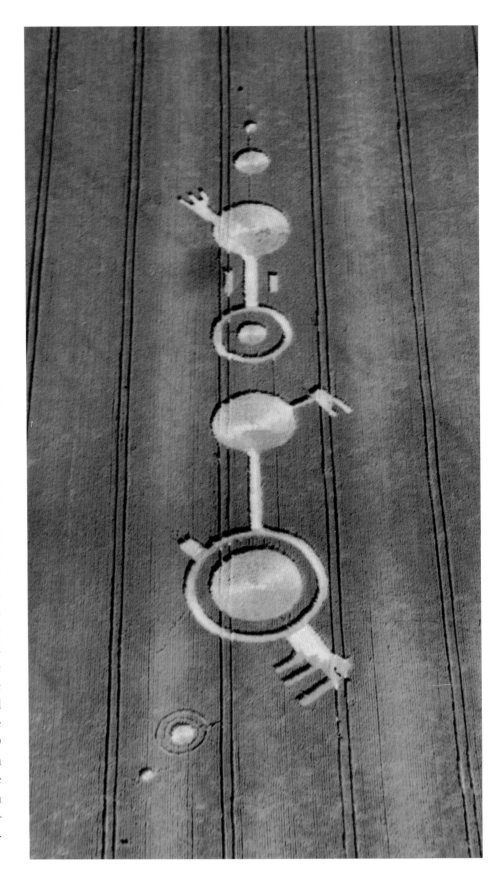

THE ONLY PROBLEM with the plasma vortex theory was that the crop circles were getting steadily more complicated in design. The first major 'pictogram' was the one which appeared at Alton Barnes in Wiltshire, UK, in July 1990 (right). It seemed unlikely that any natural phenomenon could be responsible for such a detailed and highly organized creation. By now the phenomenon had attracted many fans, all vying to solve the mystery, and over the years some weird and wonderful theories have been offered, including UFO landing sites, messages from the gods, warnings from the Earth Mother about the harm we are doing to the earth — all very spiritual and metaphysical.

A BOMBSHELL WAS dropped in September 1991 when two elderly men, Doug Bower and Dave Chorley (seen below), announced that they were responsible for the crop-circle formations. They claimed that they had been making them since the 1970s and, as the fans' fascination with the formations had grown, so they had devised ever more elaborate designs, partly to show that theories like the plasma vortex couldn't be the answer. They also claimed responsibility for the pictograms – those complex designs that people said couldn't be made by human hand. They had also invented the so-called 'insectograms', (crop formations in the shape of insects) in an attempt to show how ridiculous it all was – but they failed. Even when they confessed their guilt, many of the crop-circle enthusiasts just wouldn't believe them. By this time other hoaxers had got in on the act and, even though Doug and Dave had hung up their tools, the formations continued, getting ever more complex.

IN THE EARLY 1990s crop circles became a kind of landscape art. With each succeeding summer, the corn-artists have excelled themselves with the complexity and sheer beauty of their work. This photograph shows one of the 1996 formations, near Stonehenge. It seems impossible that such designs can be produced at night by man-power without anyone getting caught, which leads some people to hold to the belief that the major designs have a supernatural origin and that only the poorer formations are man-made. Perhaps in the near future the truth will be revealed once and for all.

ICE RINGS

THERE IS NO disputing that circles do form naturally in nature, as is proved by the occasional discoveries of ice rings. The two photographs show recent examples in the USA and in Sweden.

Right: A disc of ice 28ft (8.5m) in diameter on Cranberry Creek, at Tannersville, Pennsylvania, USA, in January 1993.

Below: A clear ring in a sheet of ice on a river in northern Sweden, in January 1987.

EARTH RINGS

CIRCULAR FORMATIONS IN the earth itself are also sometimes discovered. In the case of a crater found near Grand Coulee, Washington, USA, in October 1984, a plug of earth from the hole was found 73ft (22m) away, but no one could work out how it had been removed. The photographs show mystery holes in Russia and Canada.

Right: Two men measuring a wine-glass-shaped pit that appeared in a field in May 1990 in the Kemerovo region of Russia.

Below: A mystery depression in pasture land at New Sarepta, Alberta, Canada, found in 1992.

NATURAL FORMS AND FACES

As intelligent organisms we are constantly striving to make sense of the world around us. Bombarded with sensory stimuli, we struggle to interpret them, to match what we perceive with what is already familiar to us. So, when we see a formless shape, we attempt to 'read' it — and sometimes we are successful. Or at least, we think we are successful.

WHILE DRIVING AT dusk, I have 'seen' animals beside the road which were really plastic bags. There is not much wrong with my eyesight (except a slight deterioration due to age); it was my imagination working overtime in order to solve the mystery of the unidentified shape. Is the same tendency at work when people see the Virgin Mary in a window? The difficulty is deciding whether an image is accidental, an incorrect reading of random markings, or whether it is genuinely what it appears to be and therefore a paranormal occurrence. The photographs that follow are a mixture of the accidental and – possibly – the meaningful.

NOT MUCH IS known about the photograph below, which has been interpreted as the head of Christ among the clouds. It may have been taken in the sky over Korea, but other versions claim other origins.

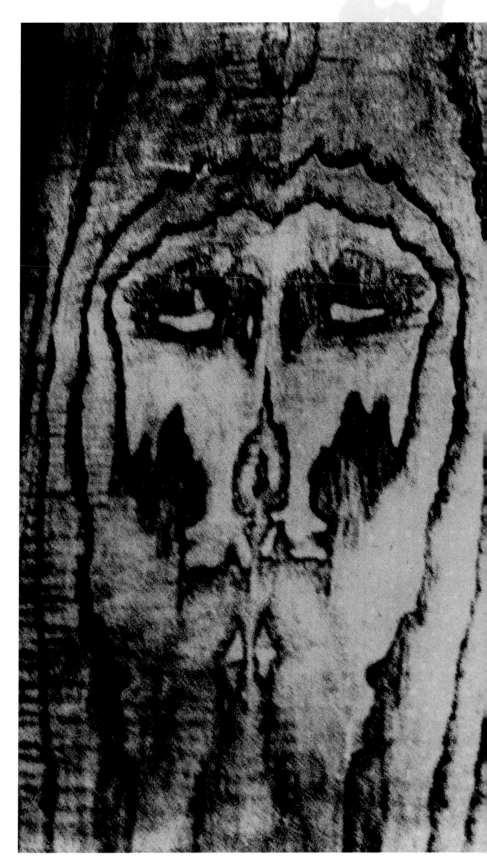

THE FACE IN a plank of wood (right) is also interpreted as being that of Christ, although in all honesty it could be anyone! There is a tendency among Christian peoples to interpret supernatural events as having religious significance, even when there is no evidence for this. Such is the case with the plank of wood. It was being used to make a kitchen cabinet when the workers, at Bacup, in Lancashire, UK, noticed that the grain of the wood resembled a face. Because this discovery was made on the same day in November 1988 as the Turin Shroud was declared a fake, someone remarked that it looked like the face on the shroud. The foreman who noticed the face commented:

> I've never seen anything like it.
> I was about to cut it when a ray
> of light shone onto the wood. I
> knew immediately it was some-
> thing special. And it appeared
> on the day experts said the
> Turin shroud wasn't authentic.
> I called my workmates over.
> They couldn't believe their eyes.

The plank later survived a fire which destroyed the premises. After the face came to light, it was reported that there was also a face of Christ (in fact 20 faces) in the wood panelling of a shoe-factory office in Bacup and it was believed to cure the sick. A partner in the firm reported that when his ulcers were hurting he would go and sit in the office for half-an-hour and the pain would go away.

RECOGNIZABLE FACES ALSO appear, on a much larger scale, in cliffs and other rocky outcrops. This example is said to be King Arthur, this identification being the natural one for a head found at Tintagel in Cornwall, where Arthur was said to have been born.

Trees and other plants can also produce recognizable human images, like the apparently sleeping woman below, in Studley Royal Park, North Yorkshire, UK.

S OMETIMES WE CANNOT be entirely sure that there has not been some paranormal force at work. In 1897, just two weeks after the death of John Vaughan, the Dean of Llandaff Cathedral in South Wales, the face of the dean appeared in a damp patch on the cathedral wall, and the letters D V could also be made out. In the early 1920s, something similar happened in Christ Church Cathedral, Oxford, UK. A face resembling that of a former dean of the cathedral, Dean Liddell, who had died in 1898, was seen on the plaster wall. The photograph below shows the image on the wall, that to the left is of the dean shortly before his death. Other faces were found nearby and yet others had appeared over the years. Shortly before Dean Liddell's face appeared, a long-lasting rift in the Liddell family had been healed and there had been a family marriage in the cathedral.

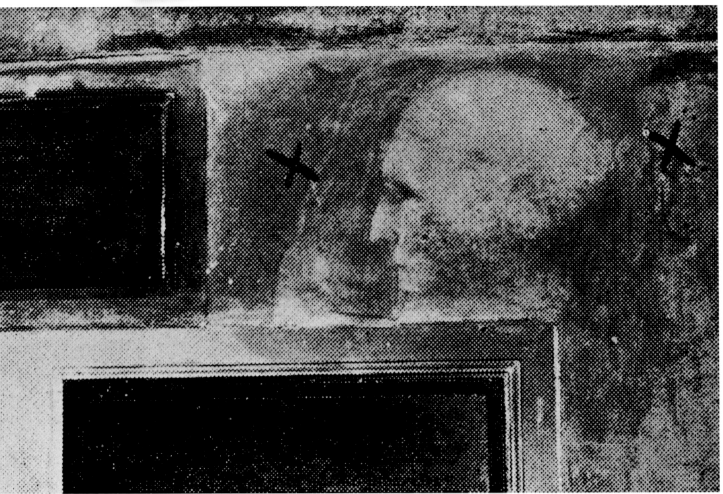

THE LARGE FACE on the right is part of a Spanish mystery going back to 1971 that has never been solved. On 23 August of that year, a peasant woman living in the village of Bélmez de la Moraleda found a face apparently painted on her kitchen floor. Six days later, the family, as a re-action to the unwelcome attention this event had brought to them, dug up the kitchen floor and replaced it with fresh concrete. A week later, Maria Pereira found another face on the floor (shown in the photograph). It stayed for several weeks, chang-ing subtly, as if the face was ageing. Eventually it was cut out of the floor and mounted behind glass. The floor was dug up and some human bones were found; the street had been built on an old graveyard. The floor was replaced again and, two weeks later, a third face appeared, and then another, this time female. A professor who was studying the faces counted 18 of them, and he was even able to watch a face forming. Nevertheless, despite intensive work by researchers, they were never able to ascertain how the faces were formed, or by whom or what. It was agreed that paranormal forces must be at work and, indeed, when tape-recorders were used in an attempt to record any 'spirits' in the house, some strange sounds were heard: loud cries, voices talking, people crying. In the early 1980s the faces started to appear again.

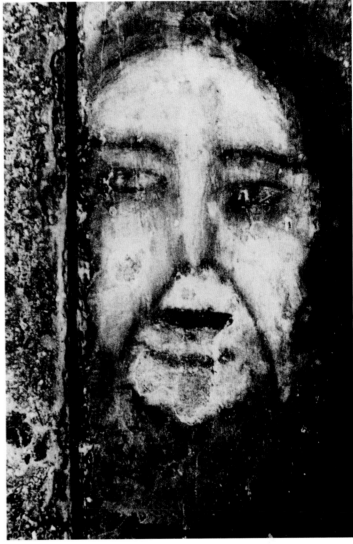

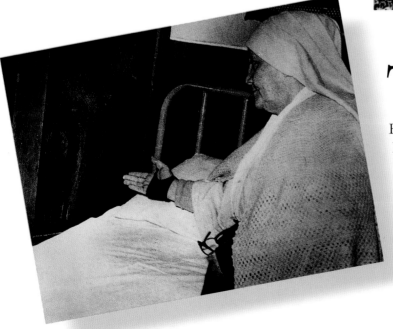

THE FACE ON the wall (left) is formed from blood and appeared in the house of the stigmatist (note her covered hands) Sister Elena Ajello (see p.125) at Cosenza, Calabria, in Italy, some time during the late 1950s. It was interpreted as being the face of Christ.

AT THE TIME of writing, the events in this final case are still on-going. They began early in 1997, soon after the Gower family bought a house and a field in Flintshire, north Wales. An Irish couple walking past the field claimed to have seen a vision of the Virgin Mary. They were standing at the field gate (left) and their vision was at the top of the steep field. Not long afterwards, Rose-Mary Gower, the field's owner, saw something strange. Her adult daughter and a friend were climbing up the field at twilight on 17 May and Mrs Gower saw three figures instead of two. The third was a hazy white 'and corresponded to my perception of what the Virgin would look like'. The vision only lasted for seconds but the girls ran downhill with the news that they had felt a presence and seen 'an undefined something'. When these happenings found their way into the media, pilgrims began to visit the field and cures were claimed by people who had stood at the gate.

Meanwhile, something else very strange was happening. A photograph of the shed standing just inside the field, taken in March, revealed possible faces on its windows, these being interpreted as resembling the face on the shroud of Turin and the Madonna, although in all truth the faces are not distinct and could be anything. If that were all, the so-called faces could be dismissed. However, a later photograph, taken at the end of May, clearly showed some letters on one of the windows: E L P or F E L E. By now, the windows were being photographed regularly and in one, taken in September, an eerie face can be seen (left). It is not possible for anyone to have stood behind the window because of the presence of bushes and brambles. The somewhat sinister air of this face caused Mrs Gower to paint crosses on both windows and the next photograph showed what could be interpreted as a figure in white robes. It is also interesting that the Gower family were experiencing some benign poltergeist phenomena in their house across the road. It is possible that the whole site is a focus for some paranormal energy forces which are expressing themselves in a variety of ways. Further developments are awaited with interest.

WEIRD STUFF THAT ISN'T: SOME MISTAKES AND SOME HOAXES

One thing is certain: only a percentage of the photographs that seem to show paranormal phenomena genuinely do so. The rest are either normal events that have been misinterpreted or outright hoaxes. The problem is: how does one categorize any photograph with any degree of certainty? The following illustrations will demonstrate some of the problems.

A T FIRST GLANCE, this photograph seems to show ghosts. The scene in India shows two glowing white figures: ghosts? In fact they were two men dressed in white clothes and head-gear, sitting directly in a shaft of sunlight which has caused them to be over-exposed in the photograph.

THIS STRANGE PHOTOGRAPH probably has a straightforward explanation. Taken in Adelaide, South Australia, in late 1975, it shows two friends chatting – but one of the men is being clasped by two apparently disembodied hands. Unfortunately the photographer won't talk about what happened, but other photographs taken at the same time show that there was also a child present, climbing about on the man at the left. Therefore, although there doesn't appear to be enough room behind the man to accommodate even a small child, logically that must be the answer.

THIS PHOTOGRAPH ILLUSTRATES a case with a message: when investigating an apparently paranormal event, retain a healthy scepticism and don't forget to look for natural explanations! In the 1980s, German parapsychologist Professor Hans Bender investigated the case of a mystery voice at a dentist's surgery in Bavaria, Germany. A rough voice, often obscene, would be heard speaking in the area of a sink. These events made sensational headlines in the newspapers for weeks, and crowds would gather outside the surgery to try and hear the voice. The dentist's 17-year-old assistant Claudia (pictured below) enjoyed appearing on television and talking about the 'ghost' who was in love with her, but Professor Bender and his colleague soon solved the mystery. With the use of hidden mirrors they proved their suspicions to be correct: Claudia was faking the voice. She was enjoying her fame and almost no longer knew what she was doing.

ALWAYS BE WARY of photographs showing streaks of light; there is almost always a straight-forward explanation. Look for a possible light source which could cause the streaks if the camera was moved while the shutter was open; this could easily happen without being noticed. This photograph actually shows streaks caused by the moon and a street lamp. The give-away is the pulsing visible on the right-hand streak; a pulsing trace is invariably caused by a street lamp.

AT FIRST SIGHT, this is a sensational photograph showing a tiny alien, allegedly from a UFO which crashed near Mexico City, USA, in the 1950s, held captive by two burly minders. In fact it is a clever hoax. It is also an old hoax. Ever since photography was discovered, skilled photographers have been able to doctor images to produce hoaxes that are hard to spot. Now that computers are available to all, the hoaxes are even more sophisticated and undetectable. The message is: never trust a photograph! The camera *can* lie.

BIBLIOGRAPHY

BOOKS

Blackmore, Susan. *Beyond the Body*. Wiliam Heinemann, London, 1982.

Bord, Janet. *Fairies – Real Encounters with the Little People*. Michael O'Mara Books, London, 1997.

Chambers, Paul. *Paranormal People*. Blandford, London, 1998.

Clark, Jerome. *Unexplained! 347 Strange Sightings, Incredible Occurrences, and Puzzling Physical Phenomena*. Visible Ink, Detroit, MI, USA, 1993.

Dash, Mike. *Borderlands*. William Heinemann, London, 1997.

Devereux, Paul, & Brookesmith, Peter. *UFOs and UFOlogy – The First 50 Years*. Blandford, London, 1997.

Evans, Hilary, & Stacy, Dennis (eds). *UFO 1947–1997 – Fifty Years of Flying Saucers*. John Brown Publishing, London, 1997. (Paperback title: *The UFO Mystery*).

Fort, Charles Hoy. *Book of the Damned*. Revised by X. Introduction by Bob Rickard. John Brown Publishing, London, 1995.

Fort, Charles Hoy. *New Lands*. Revised by X. Introduction by Jerome Clark. John Brown Publishing, London, 1996.

Fort, Charles Hoy. *Lo!* Revised by X. Introduction by John Michell. John Brown Publishing, London, 1996.

Fort, Charles Hoy. *Wild Talents*. Revised by X. John Brown Publishing, London, 1998.

Gordon, Stuart. *The Paranormal, An Illustrated Encyclopedia*. Headline Book Publishing, London, 1992.

Heuvelmans, Bernard. *In the Wake of the Sea-Serpents*. Rupert Hart-Davis, London, 1968.

Heuvelmans, Bernard. *On the Track of Unknown Animals*. Kegan Paul International, London and New York, 1995.

Heymer, John E. *The Entrancing Flame – The Facts of Spontaneous Human Combustion*. Little, Brown, London, 1996.

Huyghe, Patrick. *The Field Guide to Extraterrestrials*. New English Library, London, 1997.

North, Anthony. *The Paranormal*. Blandford, London, 1996.

North, Anthony. *The Supernatural*. Blandford, London, 1998.

Randles, Jenny. *The Paranormal Source Book – The Comprehensive Guide to Strange Phenomena Worldwide*. Piatkus Books, London, 1996.

Shuker, Dr Karl. *The Lost Ark – New and Rediscovered Animals of the Twentieth Century*. HarperCollins, London, 1993.

Shuker, Dr Karl. *In Search of Prehistoric Survivors – Do Giant 'Extinct' Creatures Still Exist?* Blandford, London, 1995.

Shuker, Dr Karl. *The Unexplained – An Illustrated Guide to the World's Natural and Paranormal Mysteries*. Carlton Books, London, 1996.

Shuker, Dr Karl. *From Flying Toads to Snakes with Wings*. Llewellyn Publications, St Paul, MN, USA, 1997.

Underwood, Peter. *Peter Underwood's Guide to Ghosts and Haunted Places*. Piatkus Books, London, 1996.

Webster, Ken. *The Vertical Plane*. Grafton Books, London, 1989.

MAGAZINES AND JOURNALS

Animals & Men – The Journal of the Centre for Fortean Zoology. Available from The Centre for Fortean Zoology, 15 Holne Court, Exwick, Exeter, EX4 2NA, UK. Tel: 01392 424811.

The Anomalist. Twice yearly. Available from Fenner Reed and Jackson, PO Box 754, Manhassett, NY 11030, USA. Internet home-page: http://www.cloud9.net/~patrick/anomalist/

Fortean Times – The Journal of Strange Phenomena. Monthly. Also as back issues bound together as books. Available from newsagents, or contact Fortean Times, FREEPOST (SW6096), Bristol, BS32 0BR, UK. Tel: 01454 620070. Fax: 01454 620080. E-mail: cihotline@aol.com Internet home-page: http://www.forteantimes.com

Fortean Studies. Annual book-length compilation of articles. Three volumes published to date. Available by mail order from Fortean Times, Unit 3, Waterloo Park, Bidford-on-Avon, B50 4JG, UK.

The Goblin Universe. Available from The Centre for Fortean Zoology, 15 Holne Court, Exwick, Exeter, EX4 2NA, UK. Tel: 01392 424811.

INFO Journal. Available from The International Fortean Organization, PO Box 367, Arlington, VA 22210-0367, USA. Internet home-page: http://www.research.umbc.edu/~frizzell/info

Strange Magazine. Twice yearly. Available from Strange Magazine, PO Box 2246, Rockville, MD 20847, USA. Tel: 301 460 4789. Fax: 301 460 1959. E-mail: strange1@strangemag.com
Internet home-page: http://www.strangemag.com

The X Factor. Cover-ups, paranormal, mysteries, UFOs. Fortnightly. Available from newsagents or by mail order. Tel: 01424 756565.
Internet home-page: http://www.xfactor.co.uk

BOOKS BY MAIL ORDER

Arcturus Books Inc., 1443 SE Port St Lucie Blvd, Port St Lucie, FL 34952, USA. Tel: 561 398 0796. Fax: 561 337 1701. E-mail: rgirard321@aol.com

Excalibur Books, Rivenoak, 1 Hillside Gardens, Bangor, Co. Down, Northern Ireland, BT19 6SJ. Tel: 01247 458579.

Midnight Books, The Mount, Ascerton Road, Sidmouth, EX10 9BT, UK. Tel: 01395 515446 (business hours and evenings, not Sundays).

Spacelink Books, Lionel Beer, 115 Hollybush Lane, Hampton, TW12 2QY, UK. Tel: 0181 979 3148.

Strange Bookshop, PO Box 2246, Rockville, MD 20847, USA. Tel: 301 881 3530. Fax: 301 460 1959. E-mail: strange1@strangemag.com
On-line catalogue: http://www.strangemag.com/bookcat.home.html

FORTEAN PICTURE LIBRARY

The Fortean Picture Library is run by us, Janet and Colin Bord, from our base in North Wales, having been founded by us in 1978. It covers all aspects of mysteries and strange phenomena, and all the photographs in this book are from the Fortean Picture Library collection.

PICTURE CREDITS

We would like to credit individual photographers as follows:

Klaus Aarsleff 114(top), 115; Larry E. Arnold 151; Yvonne Banks-Martin 168; Andrew Barker 38; Trevor Beer 36; John Billingsley 163; Dr Susan Blackmore 118, 120; John Bonar 144; The Booth Museum, Brighton 53; Borderline 161; R. Boyd 170; Kevin P. Braithwaite 107 (top); Nigel Brierly 37; Paul Broadhurst 162; Werner Burger 147; Loren Coleman 23 (top), 48 (bottom), 136, 137, 138; Eddie Coxon 62 (top); James Crocker 148; Cliff Crook 47; Rene Dahinden 18, 41, 45 (Photo Patterson/Gimlin © 1968 Dahinden), 46 (both); Haddon Davies 60; Margaret E.W. Fleming 109 (bottom); Rose-Mary Gower 166; Dr Elmar R. Gruber 84, 85 (both), 100 (both), 101 (both), 102, 103, 106 (bottom), 110 (both), 111, 114 (bottom), 126 (both), 131, 165 (top), 169; John L. Hall 143; Adam Hart-Davis 68, 77 (top), 80 (both); Austin Hepburn 17; Cynthia Hind 70–1 (all); Robert Irving 155; Peter Jordan 52, 149, 158 (top); Debbie Lee 20–1; R. Le Serrec 28; Karoly Ligeti 123 (both); Llewellyn Publications 145 (top); K.F. Lord 65; Greg Sheldon Maxwell 62 (bottom); Terence Meaden 152 (bottom), 153; John Morris 49; Christopher L. Murphy 44; S. Namiki 19; C.M. O'Connor 167; Tony O'Rahilly 59; Philip Panton 119 (bottom); Paramann Programme Laboratories 112; Guy Lyon Playfair 79, 81 (top left and bottom), 86 (both), 87, 95, 104 (both), 105 (bottom), 106 (top); Dr J.T. Richards 116 (bottom); R.J.M. Rickard 145 (bottom); Dr B.E. Schwarz 113; A.N. Shiels 16, 29; Dr Karl Shuker 39; John Sibbick and *Fortean Times* 33; SITU 40, 48 (top left and right); Bob Skinner 152 (top); Dennis Stacy 139; Derek Stafford 58, 78; Clas Svahn 158 (bottom); Busty Taylor 154, 156–7; Lars Thomas 23 (bottom), 61; Andreas Trottmann 69, 76, 77 (bottom); Ken Webster 82, 83; Zoologisches Institut, Göttingen 50 (bottom).

We are always keen to look at unusual photographs, and if you have anything interesting to offer, please send details to the Fortean Picture Library either by fax (01824 705324) or by e-mail: jbord@easynet.co.uk

INDEX